Understanding
TELECOMMUNICATIONS

Understanding
TELECOMMUNICATIONS

Ronald R. Thomas

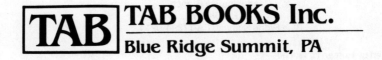

TAB TAB BOOKS Inc.
Blue Ridge Summit, PA

FIRST EDITION
FIRST PRINTING

Copyright © 1989 by TAB BOOKS, Inc.
Printed in the United States of America

Library of Congress Cataloging-in-Publication Data

Thomas, Ronald R.
    Understanding telecommunications / by Ronald R. Thomas.
        p.   cm.
    Bibliography: p.
    Includes index.
    ISBN 0-8306-3229-8(pbk.)
    ISBN 0-8306-9229-0
TK5101.T44 1988
384—dc 19   88-19940
                                                             CIP

A Petrocelli book

TAB BOOKS Inc. offers software for
sale. For information and a catalog,
please contact TAB Software Department,
Blue Ridge Summit, PA 17294-0850.

Questions regarding the content of this book
should be addressed to:

Reader Inquiry Branch
TAB BOOKS Inc.
Blue Ridge Summit, PA 17294-0214

Edited by Roman H. Gorski

Contents

To Jo Faddis

Preface

Telecommunications is a giant industry, but for most of its existence it had been a rather obscure one. From its start in the 1800s, telecommunications was best known and understood by the people who worked with it. This included technicians, operators, engineers, scientists, business people and others who made the industry grow and prosper.

In part, the unfamiliarity by the general public was due to the extensive regulation of telecommunications on both the state and Federal levels. Also, the perceived technical complexity of telecommunications kept many people from even trying to understand what it was all about.

The deregulation of telecommunications and the divestiture of the Bell System helped to give telecommunications the attention it long deserved. The ability to buy telephones in stores, to shop for long distance services, etc., all helped to increase public awareness of telecommunications.

The rise of an information society and the use of computers with telecommunications have made people even more interested in this subject. Many people are finding themselves curious about other aspects of telecommunications, including radio and television broadcasting, careers in telecommunications, etc.

This book is intended for anyone who wants an introduction to this subject. The technical material is presented in a manner that makes the book readable by any adult and by many young people, and is suitable for use in a classroom setting.

This book provides a broad overview of telecommunications using a systems approach. While specific equipment may come and go, the fundamentals presented in this book will be useful far into the future. The material will serve as a foundation for more extensive study and learning in the field of telecommunications.

I would like to thank Orlando R. Petrocelli for encouraging me to write this book and for publishing my first book, *Telecommunications for the Executive*.

Telecommunications has been a significant part of my life for over 35 years. It is a pleasure to have the opportunity to share my knowledge and love of the subject with you, the readers.

1

Development
of the Industry

ELECTRICITY
TELEGRAPH
TELEPRINTER
TELEPHONE
RADIO
AMATEUR RADIO
ELECTRONICS
TELEVISION
COMPUTERS
REGULATION
KEY WORDS
EXERCISES

This chapter considers the development of the telecommunications industry and its associated industries, primarily from an historical perspective (Table 1.1). Detailed discussions of how specific technologies work are covered in subsequent chapters. This chapter provides some feel for the flavor and texture of what has gone before and how we have arrived at today's telecommunications technology.

Many individuals and organizations played roles in the development

Table 1.1. An Historical Perspective of Telecommunications _____

1844	Samuel Morse's first telegraph message was sent between Washington, D.C. and Baltimore, MD.
1861	The first transcontinental telegraph line was placed in service between St. Joseph, Missouri and Sacramento, California.
1866	A successful telegraph cable was laid across the Atlantic Ocean.
1876	Alexander Graham Bell invented the telephone.
1892	The first automatic telephone exchange was placed in service.
1892	Chicago and New York were connected by the telephone.
1895	Guglielmo Marconi transmitted a radio signal one mile.
1901	A radio signal was transmitted across the Atlantic Ocean.
1904	The first electronic vacuum tubes were displayed.
1914	Amateur radio operators formed the American Radio Relay League.
1915	The first transcontinental telephone line between San Francisco and the East Coast was completed.
1921	Commercial radio broadcasts commenced.
1934	The Federal Communications Commission was established by Congress.
1939	Television became a practical reality.
1946	ENIAC, a large-scale electronic computer, was completed.
1950s	The transistor came into commercial use.
1950s	The computer was used in commercial applications.
1960s	Satellites were used for telecommunications applications.
1970s	Competition returned to the telecommunications industry.
1970s	Integrated circuits came into widespread use.
1984	The divestiture of the Bell System was finalized.

of this industry. It is possible in a brief chapter to mention only a few of them.

ELECTRICITY

Nothing is more fundamental to telecommunications than electricity. Without it there would not be telecommunications as we know it today (Figure 1.1), yet nothing is more difficult to explain or for most people to understand than electricity.

Electricity has become so commonplace that most people simply take it for granted. They do not bother to think about what it is or how it came into existence. Chapter 2 will discuss in some detail the more technical aspects of electricity. Here, the emphasis is on how it came into existence, some of the men behind it (and it was the nature of the time they *were* men), and some of the systems aspects of electricity.

Electricity has always existed as a force in nature. Lightning, a discharge of electricity, has always been part of our lives, but it took the minds of men to take electricity out of nature and turn it into a useful tool of society.

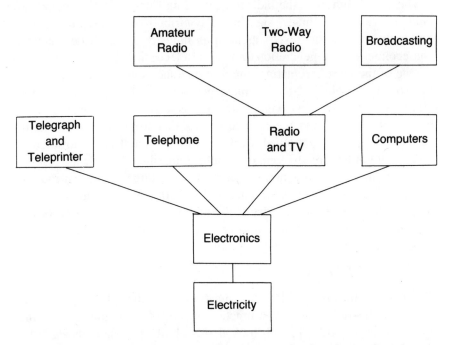

Figure 1.1. Electricity and electronics serve as the foundation for telecommunications and computers.

Everyone is familiar with Ben Franklin's kite-flying experiment. He demonstrated that lightning and electricity are one and the same. (Divine providence must have been watching over Franklin because by all rights he should have been electrocuted.)

Many other experimenters and scientists in the 1700s and 1800s were involved with electricity. Most are known only to electrical engineers and scientists, yet their names have survived in the terms given to electricity. For instance, the terms volt and voltage were named after Professor Alessandro Volta. The terms amp and amperage were named after Andre-Marie Ampère. The term watt came from the name of James Watt. All these men played vital roles in the fundamental understanding of electricity.

Others played vital roles in the development of equipment which has become an integral part of the field of electricity. Thomas A. Edison is one of the better-known names. His lightbulb is known to everyone. Edison visualized a total system for electric power, including generation, distribution and utilization. He knew that the lightbulb was just one part of the system that was needed for an economically viable industry.

There were others in the industry, including Charles P. Steinmetz and Nikola Tesla who made significant contributions. They all played important roles in the development of an industry which made practical and economical the generation and use of electricity.

One of the more fascinating things about electricity is that it moves at the speed of light—186,284 miles per second. The pioneers in the electrical field were working with speeds that took a gigantic leap beyond the human and mechanical speeds that were then common. In addition, electricity involved working with an intellectual abstraction that could not be directly seen; one could primarily view only the results.

It was the ability to generate electricity on a large scale, distribute it and produce end products which could effectively utilize it, that were the keys to creating an industry that could serve as a foundation for the field of telecommunications. It is easy to forget all that went before to make possible what is available today.

TELEGRAPH

The earliest means of telecommunications was the telegraph. It was based on electricity and was a practical means of communicating at the speed of light. The telegraph took man's ability to communicate from the speed of human or mechanical motion to the speed of light, an unprecedented leap forward.

Many individuals played roles in the development of the telegraph for communications. Most have long been forgotten. The one name which is still remembered is that of Samuel F. B. Morse who is credited with the invention of the telegraph.

Morse was a portrait painter of some repute, an unlikely individual to have invented the telegraph. It is often difficult to explain Morse and others like him who seemingly come out of nowhere to play a key role in areas that most would consider best left to scientists and engineers, but vision and creativity are not confined to any one group or profession.

Morse's first telegraph link in 1844 was between Washington, D.C. and Baltimore, MD. The success of this link proved that the telegraph could do what Morse promised. At a rapid rate, telegraph lines were laid across the U.S., the first step in wiring the nation.

Even more impressive from a technological, if not financial, standpoint was the laying of a submarine telegraph cable across the Atlantic in 1866. Cyrus Field, a merchant, was the driving force behind this enterprise.

The telegraph played a key role in the development of the U.S. in terms of commerce, industry and politics. The ability to move information at the speed of light was an important factor in the ability of a growing nation to successfully manage its expansion.

The railroads were intimately associated with the telegraph, whose lines often followed the right-of-way of the rail lines. During the Civil War the telegraph also played an important role in military communications.

However, telegraphy was a specialized field of endeavor and required trained operators. The standard telegraph apparatus was the telegraph key for sending messages and the sounder for receiving them. Among the more famous alumni of the society of telegraph operators was Thomas A. Edison, who in his younger days worked as a telegraph operator.

Morse had his name placed in history forever by the naming of the telegraph code after him. It is interesting to note that years later it was necessary to develop new codes for data communications associated with computers. So, in a sense, the telegraph code was the first means of "data communications".

Many companies played pioneering roles in the development of the telegraph industry. However, Western Union became the dominant company in the U.S. and remains so today.

Internationally, the telegraph was usually placed under the control of the government in foreign countries. Typically, the Postal Telephone and Telegraph (PTT) agencies came to control the telegraph in most foreign countries. This is still usually the case today.

TELEPRINTER

For all its glamour, often more imagined than real, the telegraph key and sounder were a rather slow method of communications, at least from a production standpoint. The system required operators who were skilled in sending and receiving Morse code. A more efficient means of sending and receiving was needed.

It came in the form of a teleprinter, often referred to as a Teletype, which is actually a trade name. A teleprinter had a typewriter-like keyboard for sending messages and a printer for receiving messages. The teleprinter permitted a skilled typist to send messages at high rates of speed without having to know the Morse code. When receiving messages, anyone could sit and watch them be printed out.

The teleprinter was more technologically complex than the telegraph key and sounder which it replaced, but the increased complexity was more than offset by the increased efficiency.

Most people never saw a teleprinter because they were typically in the back room of a telegraph office or later in the back offices of businesses. Western Union played a key role in the use of teleprinter machines by employing them in their Telex network. This was a public network for sending and receiving messages. Individuals and organizations could have direct access to it via their own teleprinter equipment. This was an interesting step forward since it meant that it was no longer necessary to go to the local telegraph office.

The Bell system also played a role in the teleprinter industry. It developed a public teleprinter network called TWX (ultimately sold to Western Union). They also created the Teletype Corporation which manufactured teleprinter equipment.

The military also used the teleprinter as a replacement for the telegraph system in many applications. Typically, the military developed their own private networks for the sending and receiving of messages, although at times they also used the public networks.

Internationally, a Telex network spanned the world. In most foreign countries it was under the control of the local government. However, thanks to international cooperation, a world-wide network of public communications using teleprinter equipment came into existence.

The general public was typically unaware of what was being done with this equipment. It was simply a back room operation that most people did not have contact with, except on rare occasions. However, it is important to remember that teleprinter communications was a viable and effective method of written message communications for both military and civilian use. It was the original electronic mail system. This is important to remember in today's era of computer-related message communications.

Teleprinter communications still exists and will be discussed in more detail in Chapter 8, which considers all forms of message communications.

TELEPHONE

It was the invention of the telephone which put telecommunications on the map. It also lead to the development of a gigantic world-wide industry.

Again it was an unlikely individual, Alexander Graham Bell, who invented the telephone. Bell was a teacher of the deaf and was actually doing work related to telegraph communications when he developed the telephone.

Another earlier pioneer in the telephone's development was Elisha Gray. Both he and Bell filed paperwork with the patent office on February 14, 1876. However, Bell filed a few hours before Gray, and it was Bell whose name eventually became synonymous with the invention of the telephone.

The ability to transmit speech was a technological marvel, and one would have thought that an eager public would have greeted its arrival. However, the public was at first slow to see the need for the telephone. This seems ironic in light of the role of the telephone in modern society.

In fact, in the early days, the telegraph industry also could not envision the telephone as competition, let alone as a real threat. Yet history would declare the telephone the winner over the telegraph.

One of the more interesting factors in the use of the telephone was that it did not require a trained operator to send or receive messages. The telephone did not require a knowledge of Morse code or the ability to type on a teleprinter. It simply required the ability to speak and listen. This was all so obvious that it simply went unnoticed.

Early telephone communications were point-to-point dedicated communications. However, it was quickly realized that the real value of the telephone was in universal communications, allowing anyone to talk to anyone.

The Bell System came to be the key player in the telephone industry. However, there were many other telephone companies in the early days of the industry. It was competitive to the extent that on occasion one company would tamper with the wires of another.

The early competition sometimes required people to have service and telephones from multiple companies, which was not an efficient method of doing business. In the U.S., the concept of a regulated monopoly was born and the Bell System became the dominant force in the industry. However, hundreds of independent telephone companies played roles in the industry. Many of them served smaller cities and towns. Today, there are approximately 1,000 independent telephone companies still in operation.

Internationally, most foreign countries chose to make the telephone an operation run by the government, typically under the Postal Telephone and Telegraph agencies. The approach in the U.S. was unique but lead to the development of a more efficient telephone system.

The impact of the telephone on the business and personal lives of everyone in the U.S. was tremendous. The telephone created an industry which employed hundreds of thousands of people. In its early days, the creation of positions for women as telephone operators opened up a whole new avenue of employment for them. Actually, the first telephone operators were often little boys, but their behavior in dealing with customers often left a great deal to be desired.

Other positions for installers, repair personnel, engineers, coordinators, managers, etc. were needed in the expanding telephone industry. Many of the positions were simply unique to the needs of the telephone industry.

RADIO

The invention of the radio provided practical telecommunications without wires, and in its early days resulted in the term "wireless communications". Guglielmo Marconi, the son of a wealthy Italian family, is the name most often associated with the development of radio. Marconi was another of those anomalies—he was not trained as a scientist or engineer. In fact, he had very little formal education.

However, in 1895, at the age of 21, he stepped out of the wings on to the stage of history by transmitting a radio signal over a mile at his parents' home in Italy. When the Italian government did not express much interest in his invention, Marconi took it to England, a maritime nation with ships and wireless communication needs.

It should be noted that scientists understood that radio communications was possible and had demonstrated it in the laboratory. However, it was Marconi who had the vision to make it into a commercial reality.

The early radio transmissions were via spark. It is difficult to imagine today what that version of radio communications was like. Sparks actually jumped between electrical contacts and the whole system was connected to a transmitting antenna. By today's standards, it is a rather crude technique, but it served for a number of years.

Radio communications relied on a telegraph key for the sending of Morse code. It was, however, a different Morse code than was used for land-based telegraph communications. The new radio code was called the International or Continental Morse code. Some operators became skilled in both codes.

It was communications with ships at sea that gave radio its commercial applications. Marconi's name became attached to a company that manufactured and operated wireless radio equipment, and for most of his life, Marconi was the driving force behind it.

One of the most difficult problems in the early days of radio communications was interference. In fact, once there were more than a few radio stations, it became a gigantic problem. It was the concept or technique of tuning that made radio a viable communications alternative. We simply take it for granted today that stations are on different frequencies on a radio or TV dial. In the early days, though, they were literally all in the same place trying to communicate.

The development of vacuum tubes gave radio a giant leap forward as a method of telecommunications, and also made voice communications a practical reality. In our era of transistors, it is important to remember that vacuum tubes were important from the early 1900s into the 1960s, and even today are used for some applications.

Many people were involved in the technological development of radio communications, but most are remembered only by professionals in the field.

The whole concept of radio and TV broadcasting was not envisioned by the early developers of radio communications. It was men like David Sarnoff, originally of the American Marconi Company and later the president of RCA, who were instrumental in the development of the broadcast industry. Sarnoff started off his career as a radio operator, but his entrepreneurial abilities moved him into the business end of the radio industry.

Today, radio communications is still used for communication with ships at sea, often via Morse code. It is also used for police and fire communications, for air traffic control, and many other applications.

AMATEUR RADIO

In the early days of radio it was all experimentation, and in a sense everyone was an amateur or experimenter. There was no such thing as licensing, frequency assignments, etc. It was all wide open for exploration and the staking out of claims.

When radio became commercialized there remained a core of dedicated amateurs for whom it remained a hobby, a method of providing emergency communications, and a technological training ground.

In the early days amateurs relied on spark communications. However, when vacuum tubes became available they transferred over to them. Voice communications also became popular with the introduction of vacuum tubes.

The commercialization of radio led some people to believe that amateurs had no further role to play in its development. In the early 1900s, amateur radio operators were assigned frequencies which were considered worthless for long distance communications. These frequencies are now called shortwave and are used for world-wide communications.

The American Radio Relay League (ARRL) was organized in 1914 and came to be and still is a primary amateur radio organization. Amateur operators built equipment, experimented, relayed emergency communications, and helped to advance the state of the radio industry. During World War II, amateur radio supplied the military with personnel who had technical training and the ability to communicate in Morse code. Many amateur operators donated their radio equipment to the military. More than one amateur radio operator entered the military service and ended up using his own equipment for military communications.

Amateur radio, often called ham radio, remained a rather obscure hobby. In part, this was due to the requirements for both technical knowledge and the ability to send and receive Morse code. Yet today there are thousands of radio amateurs all over the world, and they have continued to change with the times. While many communicate with Morse code, others use sophisticated forms of voice communications and others use teleprinters. There are even amateur communication satellites in space orbit.

It is perhaps one of the most democratic hobbies in the world. It counts among its members corporate presidents and paperboys. When communicating with each other, they are all equals.

ELECTRONICS

The development of what is now called the electronics industry has been fundamental to the development of telecommunications. Electronics can be considered to have begun with the invention of the vacuum tube. This is a somewhat arbitrary starting point, yet much of what we today call electronics started with vacuum tubes and the developments that followed.

The electronics industry also created an increase in electronic components, resistors, capacitors, etc. which were interconnected with vacuum tubes to produce a total telecommunications system. In the early days, these systems were often mounted on wooden boards and later on metal chassis.

The electronics industry is often associated with companies rather than specific individuals. General Electric, RCA and many other companies are associated with electronics.

- Of course, there are many degrees of difference among the telecommunication industries regarding their use of electronics. For example, television was totally a product of electronics, at least as a practical system. In contrast, the telephone industry used electronics but also heavily used electromechanical switching equipment and electromechanical relays.

It was the invention of the transistor in 1947 at Bell Labs that served as a significant turning point in the electronics industry. At first only a laboratory curiosity, the transistor soon laid the foundation for a revolution in electronics. Many new companies came into existence to manufacture transistor devices.

The transistor offered compactness and less heat (vacuum tubes generated significant heat and by comparison were large devices). Thus passed a certain romance to glowing vacuum tubes, just as the tubes eliminated the romance and noise of spark communications.

The development of the integrated circuit has been the most recent change in the electronics industry. It has made possible another significant reduction in the size of systems and has provided increased sophistication.

TELEVISION

It was inevitable that once man learned how to transmit the human voice through space, the next step would be to transmit full motion pictures or what is today called television.

The early experimental television techniques utilized electro-mechanical technology. In 1925, pictures were being transmitted through the air. By the late 1920s there were 15 television stations on the air in the U.S. However, the electro-mechanical systems then in use were simply not technologically sophisticated enough for the commercial market.

It was electronics which made modern-day television possible and served as the replacement for electro-mechanical systems. As in other areas of telecommunications, most of the developers of television were unknown outside of the industry.

Vladimir K. Zworykin played a key role in the development of electronic television. He had extensive college training, held a Ph.D., and for many years worked for RCA.

Philo T. Farnsworth also played a key role in the development of television. As a young man without formal technical training, he developed electronic circuits which were critical in the technological development of television. In fact, RCA Corporation ultimately had to reach an agreement with Farnsworth, the lone inventor. Farnsworth was another of those interesting individuals who step out of nowhere to play a key role in telecommunications.

It was in the broadcasting industry that television seemed destined to play its most important role. However, it took the work of giant companies like RCA and businessmen like David Sarnoff and others to make broadcast television a commercial reality.

Television required very complex electronic systems for both transmitting and receiving. It required the development of technical standards for compatibility to open up the commercial marketplace. Television also required tremendous amounts of bandwith or frequency spectrum for transmission. This necessitated agreements on frequency assignments for television stations.

World War II brought the development of television for broadcasting to a temporary halt. Resources had to be diverted to the war effort. However, at the end of the war, the push was back for the commercial development of television. In addition, there was a push for the development of color television.

It was black and white television which first invaded American homes. "A TV antenna on every roof" seemed to be the motto. Television took America by storm. It became primarily a medium for entertainment.

Again, a new industry came into existence. In a sense, it was an extension of the radio broadcasting industry. Television equipment was much more complex and it took considerable financing to put a station on the air, but the stations generated a tremendous market for television receivers.

Cable television is the most recent application of television. At first, cable systems were installed to bring television to cities and towns which were not served by local TV stations. Often they were in valleys or distant cities and could not directly access signals.

Cable television today has expanded to offer more than just distant television pictures. It can also provide channels for local news and educational programs. Frequently, cable systems can offer more channels than there are programs to fill them. Cable television is still a resource that has yet to reach its full potential.

COMPUTERS

Computers are another product that owe their existence in large measure to the electronics industry. In recent times, they have become intertwined with telecommunications.

Computers came into existence during World War II to solve—among other things—mathematical calculations related to military artillery. Among the early developers of electronic computer technology were J.V. Atanasoff, a physics professor at Iowa State University, J. Presper Eckert, Jr, and John W. Mauchly at the University of Pennsylvania. Unfortunately, the fine work of these and other early pioneers is hardly known outside of the computer industry.

ENIAC (Electrical Numerical Integrator and Calculator) is considered to be the first American electronic computer. It was developed during World War II and completed in 1946. It had 18,000 vacuum tubes and consumed over 100,000 watts of power.

At the end of the war, computers were not envisioned to have any real commercial applications of significance. Today, this is difficult to envision, just as it is difficult to envision that the telephone was not seen as having significant applications.

Even IBM was at first skeptical about a commercial future for the computer. However, they soon revised their thinking and became the giant of the computer industry.

The early computers, being dependent on vacuum tubes, were large, gave off a great deal of heat, and it took a great deal of effort to keep them operating. It was the transistor which put the computer on the map. The hot vacuum tubes were quickly replaced by the more reliable transistor, which gave off no heat and in fact had to be protected from heat. It also enabled computers to become much smaller and to do faster computations.

The development of integrated circuits, which put many electronic components on a small chip, made possible further reductions in the size of computers. It also increased their capabilities and reduced their costs. These developments kept taking place at a fantastic rate in comparison to anything that had ever happened in the past.

Large organizations were among the early users of civilian computers (airlines, banks, etc.). Almost overnight there was a whole new demand for computer professionals. The supply of trained people could not keep up with the demand.

In the early computer systems, work was physically brought to the computer. It did not take long for people to develop the ability to remotely communicate with computers via telecommunications. Thus, the power of the computer could be widely available outside of the computer room.

As the size of computers decreased, the telecommunications industry developed the concept of using computers to control telecommunications systems. One prime example was the use of specialized computers in telephone switching systems. The computer made possible a whole new generation of such systems and also helped to replace the noisy electro-mechanical systems with the quiet of computers and electronics.

Reductions in the size of computers ultimately made it possible for individuals to have personal computers at home or at work. Through computer-controlled telephone systems, these personal computers can today communicate with large computer systems at remote locations. So, today the computer is part of the telecommunications industry.

REGULATION

For most of its existence a great deal of the telecommunications industry was subject to state and Federal regulations (Table 1.2). The telephone industry came to be seen as a natural monopoly and the Bell System came to be the dominant force but under state and Federal controls. The independent telephone companies were subject to the same regulations.

On the Federal level, the Federal Communications Commission (FCC) was established by the Communications Act of 1934. The FCC became the regulator of interstate telecommunications. On the state level, the Public Service Commissions (PSC) and Public Utilities Commissions (PUC) became the local regulators.

Basically, the FCC set interstate telephone and telegraph rates. The PUC and PSC in each state regulated the rates for local service within their state.

The Bell System—through its American Telephone and Telegraph

Table 1.2. Telecommunications Regulation _____

UNITED STATES
Federal
Congress
Federal Communications Commission (FCC)
State
Public Utilities Commission (PUC)
Public Service Commission (PSC)
Federal and State
Courts

FOREIGN COUNTRIES
Postal Telephone and Telegraph (PTT)

INTERNATIONAL
International Telecommunications Union (ITU)
(voluntary agreement)

(ATT) Long Lines operation—controlled long distance telephone service in the U.S. In all fairness to Bell, it must be noted that an extensive and effective long distance network was established in the U.S. It was actually the envy of most foreign countries.

Competition after the very early years of the telephone industry ceased to exist. One telephone company, Bell or independent, served virtually every city and town in America. Long distance service all went through the Bell System. The goal was universal service for everyone, and gradually it was achieved when most everyone came to have a telephone. Along with this goal there was a philosophy of permitting one service to subsidize another. As a result, long distance revenues helped to keep down the cost for local service.

Internationally, telephone and telegraph regulation was handled differently. In most foreign countries the government ran the telephone and telegraph systems. Typically, this was done through PTT agencies.

There were also organizations which did not have direct control but served as coordinators. Among the better known is the International Telecommunications Union (ITU) headquartered in Switzerland. The ITU developed standards for international communications among countries through voluntary agreement by each country.

When the broadcasting industry came to be a significant force in the U.S., its regulation ultimately came under the FCC. What the FCC was really doing was allocating a scarce resource, specific frequencies or channels in the broadcast spectrum.

The broadcasting industry is a more visible and glamorous industry than the telephone industry and usually receives much more of the public's attention. Broadcasting is also more competitive, since multiple radio and TV stations typically serve the same city.

The electronics industry basically remains unregulated. Anyone can make electronic components, equipment, receivers, etc. There is some Federal regulation of transmitting equipment to ensure that certain technical standards are met, but by comparison to the telecommunications industry which uses the electronic equipment, this regulation is minimal.

It was the deregulation of the telecommunications industry, particularly of the telephone industry in the late 1960s, that changed the nature of this business. It was an unlikely individual, Tom Carter, who challenged the status quo of the industry. He operated a small company in Texas, and on his own initiative he challenged the Bell monopoly and won.

Deregulation moved at a rapid pace and lead in 1984 to the divestiture of the Bell System. No one can be the judge of how it will all work out, but competition and the divestiture have certainly opened up the marketplace to many new vendors.

The broadcasting industry has seen some deregulation in terms of the licensing of operators of broadcasting equipment. However, the basic nature of the limited frequency assignments and the necessity to prevent interference between stations, limit the degree to which deregulation is possible.

It is fascinating to see how telecommunications has gone full circle from the early days of total competition to regulation and now a return to significant deregulation and the return of competition.

KEY WORDS

The reader should be familiar with the following terms in the context in which they were used in this chapter:

Amateur radio

Bell System

Broadcasting

Computers

Electricity

Electronic components

Electronics

ENIAC

FCC

Frequency

Independent telephone companies

Integrated circuits

ITU

PSC

PTT

PUC

Radio

Regulation

Speed of light

Telegraph

Telephone

Teleprinter

Television

Transistor

Tuning

Vacuum tubes

EXERCISES

1. Why is electricity of such importance to telecommunications?

2. What major advantage did the telegraph offer over previous methods of communication?

3. How did the teleprinter simplify message communications?

4. Discuss the impact of the telephone on society.

5. Give three advantages of radio communications.

6. What functions have been provided by amateur radio?

7. Discuss three of the most significant advances in the electronics industry.

8. What is a major technical disadvantage of television?

9. How did broadcasting come into existence?

10. What two roles have computers played in telecommunications?

11. Name the primary regulating agencies of telecommunications.

12. How did individuals with limited formal training or credentials manage to play key roles in the development of telecommunications?

2

Electricity and Electronics

This chapter considers electricity and electronics, both fundamental to telecommunications. Electricity is a mature industry with many clearly established principles. The electronics industry is clearly established but has experienced many changes over the years.

Electricity and electronics are often described in mathematical terms. This chapter will rely primarily on words to convey an understanding of both concepts. This will at times oversimplify the material being presented, but the intent is to provide a basic understanding to the widest possible range of readers.

By understanding the fundamentals in this chapter, the reader will have a much better ability to understand what goes on inside telecommunications equipment and systems. The mythical "black box" will be much less mystical.

DIRECT CURRENT

Direct current (DC) is one type of electricity. It is also one of the oldest varieties of practical electricity. Static electricity, which is generated as a person walks across a carpet on a cold winter day, is an even older form of electricity, but is not suitable for practical applications.

Electricity depends on the movement of electrons which are part of the atom. It is not necessary to be a physicist to grasp the concept of a movement of electrons. They are simply small particles that cannot be seen. To help simplify our thinking about this, the flow of electricity is frequently described as being similar to the flow of water. This helps to make the subject a little less abstract.

There are some basic terms which are used to describe electricity. The first is the term "volt". Everyone has heard it used. An automobile battery is described as being a 12-volt battery. The electricity in homes is described as being 120 volts. The volt can be thought of as a way of describing electrical pressure. The greater the number of volts, the greater the electrical pressure.

The term "amp" can be thought of as a measure of the volume of the electrical flow. In automobiles there are fuses or circuit breakers. These devices are described in terms of their amps or amperage. The greater the amp rating, the more current that can flow through them. However, when the rating is exceeded or the flow is too great, the fuse or breaker stops all electrical current flow. This is a safety measure to prevent fires.

The term "watt" is a way of talking about electrical power. It is a function of volts and amps. Lightbulbs are rated in terms of watts. A 150-watt bulb gives off more light than a 75-watt bulb but it also uses more amps, the volts being a constant.

Direct current, as the name implies, always flows in the same direction. This is in contrast to alternating current which will be described in the following section. Direct current is what Edison worked with in developing the lightbulb. It is still used today in flashlights, automobiles, and in electronic equipment which will be described later.

There are certain substances, known as conductors, which easily permit the flow of electricity. The most common is copper wire, used in home and automobile wiring and in electronic and telecommunications equipment.

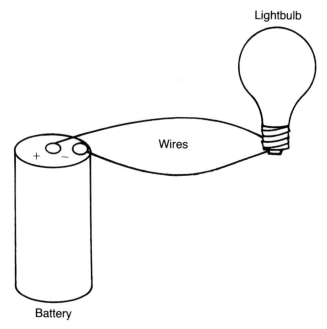

*Figure 2.1. A simple direct current electrical circuit. The electricity flows
from the battery through the wires to the bulb.* _____

There are other substances, known as insulators, which do not permit
the flow of electricity. Plastic, for example, does not conduct electricity
and so is an insulator.

A lightbulb connected to a battery with copper wire is a simple direct
current electrical circuit (Figure 2.1). The battery produces electricity at
a certain voltage to light the bulb. The battery and bulb are connected in
a direct current circuit.

Christmas tree lights in the past were wired in series (Figure 2.2). If
one light failed, the whole string of lights would go out. Each light had
to be tested to detect the one that had failed.

There is another type of electrical circuit in which the elements are
connected in parallel with the power source (Figure 2.3). The present
generation of Christmas tree lights, which continue to work even if one
or more lights fail, are wired in parallel. Electricity flows through each
light at the same time and the failure of one or more lights does not
affect the remaining lights.

There are devices which can be used to measure electricity, the meter
being the most common one. A meter can visually show various electri-

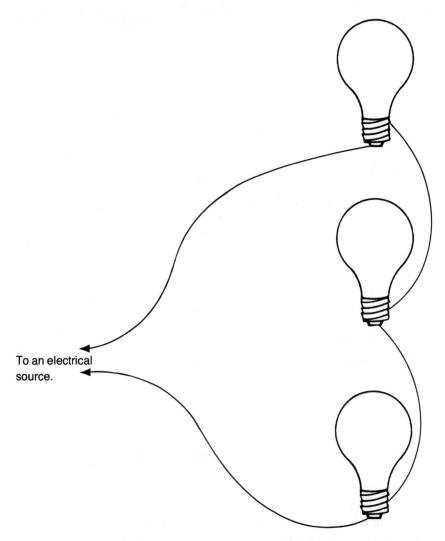

Figure 2.2. A series electrical circuit. The electricity has to have a path through all three lightbulbs. The failure of one light will cause all of the lightbulbs to remain dark. _____

cal parameters; for example, voltmeters show how much voltage is present. An ampmeter shows the volume of the electrical flow. A wattmeter shows how much power is being consumed.

Mathematical formulas can also be used to calculate electrical parameters. One of the most fundamental direct current electrical formulas is

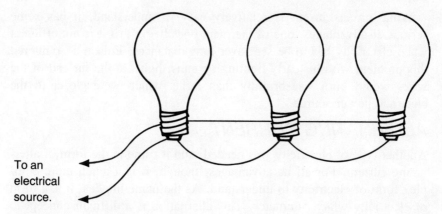

To an
electrical
source.

Figure 2.3. A parallel electrical circuit. The failure of one or two lightbulbs will not prevent the remaining bulb(s) from remaining lit. They all have equal access to the electricity. _____

Ohm's law, developed in 1827 by George Simon Ohm, a German school teacher (Figure 2.4). It is based on a relationship between electrical voltage, amperage and resistance. The term "resistance" is used to describe opposition to the flow of electricity by a substance.

There are many other mathematical formulas, rules and laws used to describe electricity. They are all part of what is called basic electrical theory.

<u>OHM'S LAW</u>

$$I = \frac{V}{R}$$

I is the current in amps

V is the voltage in volts

R is the resistance in ohms

Figure 2.4. Ohm's law in the form of a mathematical formula states that the amount of current in amps in a direct current circuit is directly proportional to the voltage in volts and inversely proportional to the resistance in ohms. _____

While direct current is relatively easy to understand, it has some serious disadvantages, one of the main ones being that it is not efficient when electricity has to be sent over long distances. Edison encountered this problem with his early lighting systems; lights at the far end of the wires would burn less brightly than lights which were closer to the electrical power source.

ALTERNATING CURRENT

Another type of electricity was needed, and it came in the form of alternating current. For all its advantages, though, it is a much more complex form of electricity to understand. As the name implies, it is a form of electricity which alternates. This alternation is a difficult concept to understand.

Usually, alternating current is described in mathematical terms. It was men with extensive mathematical training, like Charles Steinmetz and Nikola Tesla, who were among the pioneers in the development and application of alternating current. Men who were not mathematically oriented, and this included Edison, had a difficult time grasping the concept of alternating current.

In fact, when alternating current first came into existence, the proponents of direct current felt that it was a very dangerous form of electricity. The proponents of alternating current tried to stress its inherent efficiencies. For a period of time, there was an electricity "war," the war of the currents.

Alternating current alternates back and forth. The alternations are described in terms of frequency or how often they occur. The alternating current in houses in the U.S. normally alternates at 60 Hertz (cycles) per second. (The term "Hertz" is used in place of cycle. This is to pay respect to Heinrich Hertz, a German physicist of the 1800s who played a pioneering role in the electrical field.)

The term "sine wave" is also used to describe the changes of alternating current (Figure 2.5). The sine wave starts at zero, rises to a maximum positive value, goes back to zero, then goes to a maximum negative value, and finally goes back again to zero. At the zero point, the alternation process starts all over again.

This concept becomes more complex when the term "phase" is introduced. Phase refers to the relationship of sine waves to each other. It is described in terms of degrees (Figure 2.6).

The significance of phase is that in an alternating current circuit, unlike direct current, the voltage and amperage can be out of phase with each other. This further serves to explain why alternating current is

A SINE WAVE

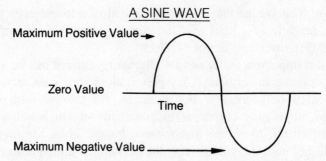

Maximum Positive Value ➔

Zero Value

Time

Maximum Negative Value ➔

Figure 2.5. Shown is one complete cycle of an alternating current. It goes from zero to a maximum positive value then back to zero and to a maximum negative value and then back to zero, where the process can start all over again. _____

difficult to understand and why it is necessary to use mathematics to describe it.

Alternating current can be measured with meters. Volts and amps are again used as a measure of alternating current. Since the intensity of alternating current is constantly changing, as shown by the sine wave, the measurements can give only an approximate value. For example, the voltage might be described in terms of its peak value or some average value.

There are a number of practical reasons for the use of this form of electricity. The first is that it is very suitable for transmission over long

MULTIPLE SINE WAVES

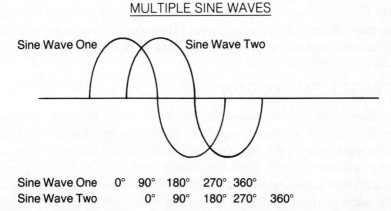

Sine Wave One   Sine Wave Two

Sine Wave One	0°	90°	180°	270°	360°	
Sine Wave Two		0°	90°	180°	270°	360°

Figure 2.6. Shown are two sine waves which are out of phase with each other, in this example by 90 degrees. Phase differences are a common occurrence in alternating current circuits. _____

distances. This means that a light at the end of a long electric wire can glow as brightly as a light near the power source. This is important in the long distance transmission of electricity.

Another important factor is that alternating current can be used with devices called transformers. They permit alternating current voltages to be increased or decreased. For example, for transmission over long distances, alternating current is increased to very high voltage levels, via transformers, to reduce transmission losses. Then, via transformers at the distant end, the voltage is reduced (stepped down) before it enters a house or place of business. Thousands and hundreds of thousands of volts are used for long distance transmissions of electricity. However, this voltage is reduced to 120 volts for use in homes and other places. These lower voltage levels help to reduce the danger of electrical shock.

So, for all its complexity, alternating current is a primary form of electricity. Alternating current is also widely used in other parts of the world. However, the voltage standard may be different than that in the U.S. In some countries, 220 volts is the standard. The frequency in foreign countries is often 50 Hertz rather than the 60 Hertz found in the U.S. So, tourists in other countries often take voltage converters to permit their electric razors, hair dryers, etc. to operate on the local voltage.

Even in the U.S., other voltage levels are often used. In many homes, large electrical appliances such as stoves and air conditioners often use voltages higher than 120 volts. This typically requires the installation of a special electrical outlet for each appliance.

Some industrial plants also routinely use voltages higher than 120 volts. These higher voltages (220 volts, 440 volts, etc.) are often needed to operate large electrical equipment. However, alternating current is very flexible, and due to transformers it can be adapted to a multitude of needs.

POWER GENERATION

The original source of man-made electricity were batteries which— through chemical reactions—produced direct current. Batteries are still widely used today, and are often called dry cells. This is to contrast them to a wet cell, such as an automobile battery.

If a dry cell is cut open, inside will be seen a solid or pasty substance. A car battery, however, has a mixture of water and acid. Neither type should be casually opened or played with, since they both contain chemicals.

Batteries usually provide low voltage levels. A standard flashlight battery is rated at 1.5 volts. Car batteries are usually rated at 12 volts. In the past, car batteries were only 6 volts. The 12-volt batteries are needed to power all of the electrical devices now found in modern automobiles. The 12-volt battery also makes it easier to start a car on cold winter mornings.

Alternating current is normally generated at a power plant and brought into cities via high voltage electrical transmission wires. This generation is done by converting mechanical energy into electrical energy. This is possible because the movement of a wire through a magnetic field produces electricity. Electrical generators, through mechanical motion, rotate coils of wire in a magnetic field and the result is the generation of electricity. By way of contrast, a motor is a device which takes electricity and converts it into mechanical motion.

Magnetism exists as a force within nature. There are natural magnets called lodestones, which are mineral magnets. When electricity was first discovered, it was not known that it has a relationship to magnetism. The discovery of this relationship made possible the generation of electricity on a large scale and in an economical manner.

Electric power plants generate electricity on a grand scale using very large generators. One of the oldest methods of supplying the energy to rotate these generators is to use the movement of water. Niagara Falls is an example of this concept.

Another way to generate electricity on a large scale is to use steam to rotate an electrical generator. Coal is often used to heat the water and turn it into steam. Nuclear energy can also be used as a replacement for coal to heat the water. The electrical energy does not come directly from the nuclear energy source.

Once the energy in the form of electricity is generated, it is necessary to distribute it to the end-users (Figure 2.7). This is done through the use of transformers and high voltage transmission lines. The voltage is stepped up at the generation site and stepped down at the distant end.

Many devices operate directly from alternating current. This includes electric irons, stoves, etc. However, electronic and telecommunications equipment normally converts alternating current into direct current. It is the nature of such equipment that they need direct current.

A device called a power supply converts alternating current into direct current through a process called rectification. A home television has a built-in power supply to convert alternating current into direct current.

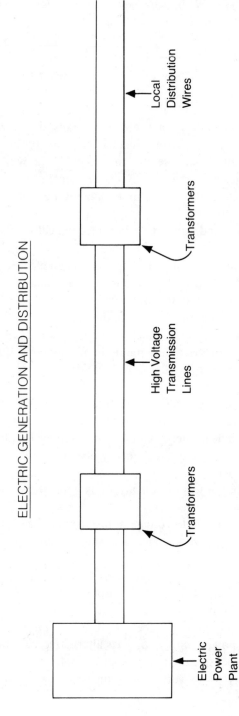

ELECTRIC GENERATION AND DISTRIBUTION

Electric Power Plant

Transformers

High Voltage Transmission Lines

Transformers

Local Distribution Wires

Figure 2.7. Electricity is generated at a power plant where transformers increase the voltage to high levels for long distance transmission. At the distant end, transformers decrease the voltage for local distribution to homes and businesses.

Many different levels of direct current are used in electronic and tele-communications equipment. The voltages could range from only a few volts in transistor devices to hundreds of volts in tube devices.

Electricity is dangerous to human beings and other forms of life because it can interfere with bodily functions, particularly the proper operation of the heart. It can also cause serious burns. Since electricity cannot be directly seen, any electrical wire has to be approached with caution.

Why can birds sit on electrical power wires and not be hurt? They only have contact with one wire. If they could have contact with two wires or the ground at the same time, they would get an electrical shock.

People who routinely work with electricity have learned to have a healthy respect for it. They check that equipment has been disconnected from the power source before they work on it. They try to stand on insulating material when working with the equipment. This helps to reduce the possibility of an electrical shock if they do come in contact with an electrical power source. People who work around power lines routinely wear insulating gloves and take every precaution to avoid coming in contact with wires which are carrying electricity.

Yet every year people are accidently killed by electricity. This includes those killed by lightning which is a very dangerous form of electricity. One of the safest places to be in an electrical storm is in an automobile, which is insulated from the ground by rubber tires.

VACUUM TUBES

In an age of transistors and integrated circuits, it is easy to forget that vacuum tubes were their precursor for many years. As they still play a role in modern-day electronics and telecommunications, an understanding of how they work is important.

It was Thomas Edison who was first associated with what ultimately became the vacuum tube. In his work with lightbulbs, he noticed that the glass of the bulb would sometimes become darkened. While he noted this in his laboratory records, he did not follow up on it. (It was others—including J. A. Fleming of England and Lee deForest of America—who played key roles in the actual development of the vacuum tube.) The effect which Edison noted was caused by electrons being burned off the hot filament of the lightbulb. This is the Edison Effect.

It was the introduction of another element, called a plate, which produced the first vacuum tube. The two-element vacuum tube is called a diode.

In a diode vacuum tube, a positive voltage of direct current is placed on the plate. It serves to attract the electrons which have a negative charge and are given off by the hot filament. It is an electrical law that positive and negative attract.

It was the introduction of a third element, called a grid, which produced the triode vacuum tube and put the vacuum tube on the map forever (Figure 2.8). A grid is a wire mesh through which electrons flow on their way to the plate. A positive electrical voltage on the grid can speed up the flow of electrons to the plate and a negative voltage on the grid can slow the flow down.

The grid permits a rather weak voltage on it to have a significant impact on the electron flow. This is fundamental to the operation of the vacuum tube. It permits, among other things, a weak radio signal to be

VACUUM TUBE

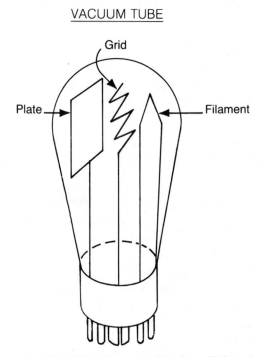

Figure 2.8. Shown is a three-element vacuum tube called a triode. The three elements are connected to pins in the base via wires. Vacuum tubes are designed to be plugged into sockets. _____

picked out of the air and converted into sound loud enough to operate a loudspeaker.

The first vacuum tubes greatly resembled lightbulbs. The various elements could easily be seen within the glass bulb. The glowing filament gave off both heat and light. A number of vacuum tubes would quickly become a source of usually unwanted heat.

The early vacuum tubes operated totally on direct current. It was the introduction of another element called a cathode which permitted vacuum tube filaments to be powered directly by alternating current. The cathode is a metal tube which surrounds the filament, and when heated it gives off electrons. The direct current was frequently obtained from the two-element vacuum tubes through the process of rectification. (This process will be described further under the section on electronic circuits.)

Tubes with additional elements came into existence and also found widespread use. The development of television saw the need for a very large vacuum tube to be used as the television picture tube. Similar types of picture tubes are used today for the display screens of personal computers. In fact, picture tubes are used in test equipment and radar systems.

High-powered radio and television transmitters still use vacuum tubes to generate radio and TV signals. However, even these tubes may eventually be replaced by transistors.

ELECTRONIC COMPONENTS

For all of their importance, vacuum tubes could not have functioned without other electronic components. Some understanding of these components is helpful in understanding how electronic circuits and telecommunications equipment function.

Symbols are used to represent the various types of electronic components (Figure 2.9). These symbols are combined to produce electrical diagrams which will be discussed in the following section on electronic circuits.

A common electronic component is the resistor. Typically, resistors are small pieces of carbon with a wire protruding from each end. There are also resistors made up totally of wire and not carbon. As the name implies, a resistor serves to resist the flow of electricity.

Insulators are resistors of such high value that the flow of electricity is completely stopped. However, resistors normally limit but do not totally stop the flow of electricity.

ELECTRONIC COMPONENT SYMBOLS

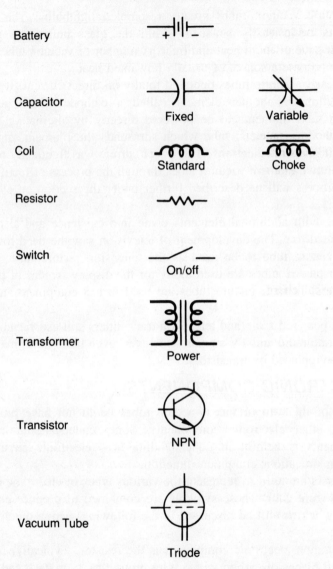

Battery

Capacitor

Fixed   Variable

Coil

Standard   Choke

Resistor

Switch

On/off

Transformer

Power

Transistor

NPN

Vacuum Tube

Triode

Figure 2.9. Shown are some of the commonly-used electronic component symbols. These are combined to produce schematic diagrams which illustrate entire electronic circuits.

A simple example will help to explain how a resistor can be used. An old six-volt car radio could operate in a new 12-volt car by using a resistor which resists six of the volts. Actually, six of the 12 volts is consumed in the resistor, leaving only six volts for the old car radio.

In electronic and telecommunications equipment, resistors play a more sophisticated role in conjunction with other electronic components. One of the more common of these components is the capacitor (formerly called a condenser).

A capacitor is a device which can store electricity. Capacitors consist of conducting material separated by insulating material. This may be metal foil separated by insulating paper. From both ends protrudes a wire, similar to a resistor.

The tuning dial in a radio is often a variable capacitor. It consists of metal plates which are insulated from each other by an open space. Turning the dial moves one set of plates between the second set of plates; however, they never touch.

Capacitors, like resistors, come in various sizes. Large capacitors are often found in the power supplies of electronic equipment, and can hold an electrical charge for a long period of time. In fact, even after the capacitor is disconnected from a power source, it can still give off electricity and shock or even kill someone careless enough to touch it. Technicians routinely discharge such capacitors before they work on equipment.

Another electronic component is the coil. A coil is typically wire wrapped around some type of insulating material. The size of a coil and the number of turns of wire all determine the electrical value of a coil.

Coils are often used in combination with capacitors. This can produce a circuit which is most effective at a certain radio frequency or place on the radio dial. For example, the variable capacitor in a radio is typically connected to a coil. Rotating the capacitor changes its value and in turn changes the frequency at which the coil and capacitor are most effective. The net result is the selection of various radio stations.

Another use for coils, called choke coils, is to oppose the flow of alternating current. Inductance is the name given to the property of a coil to oppose a change. Such coils are important in electronic and telecommunications equipment.

Transformers are devices which have multiple coils of wire wrapped around a metal core, and permit the value of electrical voltage to be changed. They work on alternating current. Direct current through a coil of wire around a metal core would produce an electromagnet.

An alternating current through the winding of a transformer produces a changing magnetic field which affects the other windings. This is what makes the transformer work. The metal core makes the transformer more efficient. There are also devices which have multiple coil windings, operate at radio frequencies, and do not have metal cores. They are used to transfer radio energy only.

Other electronic components are often found in electronic and telecommunications equipment. For example, the volume control on a radio and TV set is normally a variable resistor. By rotating it, the value of resistance is changed and along with it the intensity of the sound.

Switches are another common electronic component. They serve a number of functions. One of the most common is to stop the flow of electricity. An on/off switch opens and closes electrical contacts and permits or prevents the flow of electricity. A light switch does the same thing to control a lightbulb.

There are other switches, such as band switches which are used in multiband radios. A band switch has multiple electrical contacts which connect to coils, capacitors, etc. Rotating the switch selects various alternate coils and capacitors to change the band being received.

ELECTRONIC CIRCUITS

In the early days, vacuum tubes were the heart of electronic circuits. However, it was the total combination of vacuum tubes with resistors, capacitors, coils, etc. which produced an electronic circuit.

The early electronic circuits were often easier to understand because they were commonly mounted on a wooden board. A person could see all the physical components and how they were connected together.

Gradually, the metal chassis replaced wooden boards as a mounting device. Underneath the metal chassis were the components. The vacuum tubes stuck out of the chassis on the top side.

The metal chassis was replaced by the printed circuit board. It still contained sockets for vacuum tubes, and the components were mounted on the board. However, printed wiring replaced the physical wires which had been used previously. All of these changes in mounting methods were steps in simplifying and improving the manufacturing of equipment.

Normally, on a metal chassis or printed circuit board, there were multiple electronic circuits which combined to produce a radio receiver, transmitter, etc. When these devices were intended for use in the home, they had nice wooden cabinets to make them look like pieces of furniture.

It is helpful to understand a few of the basic electronic circuits and how they are combined to produce a total system. One of the most basic of these circuits is the power supply. It typically consists of a power transformer to convert 120-volt alternating current into some other voltage level. Vacuum tubes or transistors convert the alternating current to pulsating direct current (semi-direct current), and then choke coils and large capacitors smooth out the electrical flow and produce pure direct current. Power supplies are commonly used today in computers, telecommunications and electronics equipment.

Another common electronic circuit is the oscillator. It uses capacitors, coils, tubes or transistors to create a circuit capable of generating a radio signal. Oscillator circuits are fundamental to radio and TV transmitting equipment. They are also used in receiving equipment and computers, which need low-power radio signals used only internally to accomplish other electronic functions.

Another electronic circuit is the detector. It uses vacuum tubes or transistors and other electronic components to produce a circuit which can convert radio energy into audio energy. Such circuits are used in radio receivers which intercept radio signals and produce audio signals which can be heard by the human ear.

The amplifier circuit is also widely used in electronic and telecommunications equipment. Vacuum tubes or transistors combined with resistors, capacitors, etc. produce a circuit which will take a weak signal and make it stronger. This can be done for both audio and radio signals. A public address system is made up of amplifying circuits.

The invention of the computer created a need for special electronic circuits. One such circuit is the gate. It uses transistors, resistors, capacitors, etc. to produce a circuit fundamental to computer operations.

As the name "gate" implies, this circuit permits certain specific things to happen on its output depending on what is happening on its input. There are different types of gate circuits just as there are different types of oscillators, amplifiers, etc.

All of these various circuits can be combined to produce electronic, computer, and telecommunications systems. These circuits and systems can be represented on schematic diagrams that show the components and wiring symbolically. Schematic diagrams are routinely used for the installation and repair of electronic equipment (Figure 2.10).

The connecting of circuits produces telecommunications systems. An illustration will help to clarify this concept. A simple one-tube radio set can be made using only a simple detector circuit. The resulting signal is strong enough to only be heard with earphones. By adding an audio amplifying circuit the sound could be played through a speaker. By

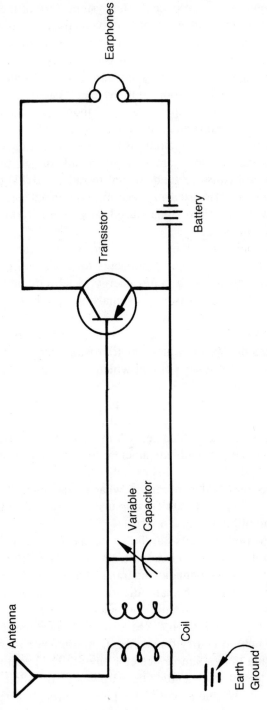

Figure 2.10. A schematic diagram of a one-tube radio receiver. Symbols are used to represent physical components.

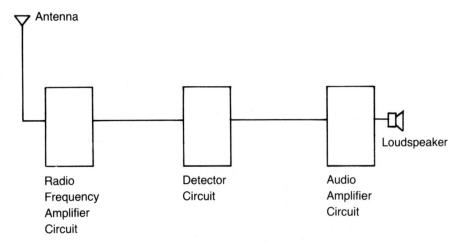

Figure 2.11. Block diagram of a radio set using multiple electronic circuits which produce sophisticated telecommunications systems. _____

placing a radio frequency amplifier circuit between the detector circuit and the antenna, weak radio signals could be received. (Figure 2.11).

This same principle is used to create complex electronic and computer systems. Even when transistors, integrated circuits, etc. are involved in modern systems, this same basic principle of combining circuits still holds true. It is fundamental to the electronics industry.

TRANSISTORS

The transistor has become the widespread replacement for the vacuum tube. Transistors are often called solid-state devices. They are produced using materials called semiconductors (germanium, silicon, etc.).

Transistors are sometimes seen as more difficult to understand than vacuum tubes. This is due in part to the fact that transistors are so small that their internal parts cannot be seen. The transistor created a revolution because of its small size, low electrical power consumption, and the fact that it does not give off heat. The transistor made possible tremendous reductions in the size of electronic and telecommunications equipment.

A basic transistor can be thought of as being similar to a simple vacuum tube (Figure 2.12). The transistor has an emitter which is analogous to the filament of a vacuum tube. The base is analogous to the grid of the vacuum. The collector is analogous to the plate of a vacuum tube.

Transistors also depend on the flow of electrons. However, unlike the vacuum tube which requires a hot filament to produce electrons, the

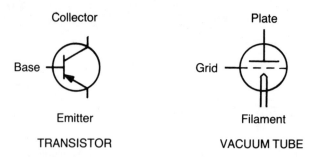

Figure 2.12. On the left is the symbol for a transistor and on the right is the symbol for a vacuum tube. The various elements are somewhat analogous to each other.

transistor needs only very low direct current voltages to produce an electron flow through the semiconductor materials of which it is composed.

The movement of electrons from the emitter to the collector can be affected by the base of the transistor. The result is a device which can perform the same type of functions as a vacuum tube but without the disadvantages of a vacuum tube (Figure 2.13).

There are different types of transistors—junction transistors, field-effect transistors, unijunction transistors and others. They all serve to perform various functions previously performed by vacuum tubes.

The early transistors were capable of handling only very low power levels. Later, larger and more powerful transistors came into existence which can handle the higher power levels found in some radio transmitters, audio amplifiers, etc.

While small transistors are cold to the touch, large transistors have noticeable heat. These transistors have metal cases and metal plates to help dissipate the heat.

The small size of transistors made it more cost effective to mount electronic circuits and whole systems on printed circuit boards. The computer industry was particularly affected by the size reductions made possible by transistors. Rather than having 18,000 vacuum tubes in a computer that took up a whole room, the transistor led the way to smaller computers.

Transistors have been valuable in other aspects of electronics and telecommunications. Small portable television cameras and receivers are based on transistor technology. Telephone switching systems utilize the transistor for replacing larger electromechanical devices that produce noise, are affected by dirt, etc.

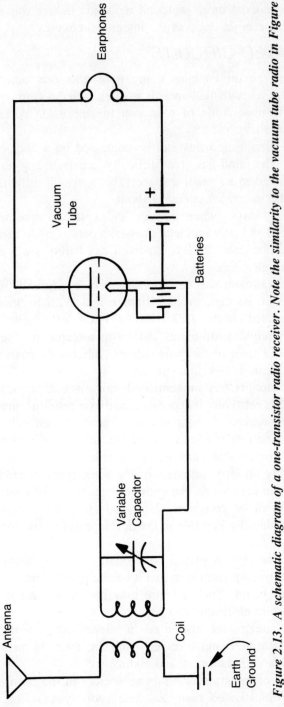

Figure 2.13. A schematic diagram of a one-transistor radio receiver. Note the similarity to the vacuum tube radio in Figure 2.10.

However, an even more profound reduction in size was in the making, and it came in the form of the integrated circuit.

INTEGRATED CIRCUITS

An integrated circuit contains many transistors and other electronic components in a very small area. It is often called a chip. It is difficult to explain the magnitude of reduction in size made possible by the integrated circuit.

A million circuit elements can be contained on a chip one-quarter-inch square. The mind has great difficulty understanding how so much can be contained in so small a space. This makes it difficult to understand what the integrated circuit is about.

In the early days, when circuits and systems were mounted on wooden boards and later on metal chassis, a person could clearly see the individual components. Today, a person can barely see a chip with a million circuit elements.

Just as the transistor was developed by people—actually three men at Bell Labs (John Barden, Walter Brattain and William Shockley)—so was the integrated circuit. Jack Kilby of Texas Instruments and Robert Noyce of Fairchild Instruments did basic research on the integrated circuit and hold some of the basic patents. Other individuals also played important roles in its development.

Integrated circuits rely on semiconductor material, typically silicon. This material is relatively inexpensive, and as a result integrated circuits have become relatively inexpensive to produce and sell. Integrated circuits are often referred to as part of the "silicon revolution".

It is in computers that integrated circuits have found widespread use. Computers rely on large numbers of the same types of circuits, gates, etc., to perform their work. An entire computer can be contained on an integrated circuit or computer chip. Ted Hoff, an engineer at Intel Corporation, played a key role in the development of the computer on a chip.

Typically, the chip is placed on a small mounting board which has metal pins protruding from it so that it can be plugged into a socket on a printed circuit board. Such a board may have a number of integrated circuits and other electronic components on it.

Integrated circuits are also used in telecommunications equipment including transmitters and receivers, and are used for many sophisticated functions such as tuning and control.

The impact of integrated circuits on society in the form of personal computers, sophisticated radio and television systems, etc. has been tremendous. The impact on engineers and technicians has also been profound. An engineer or technician who started to work in 1950 was trained to use vacuum tubes. By 1980, he or she would have had to have been retrained to understand transistors and then integrated circuits.

While it is difficult to predict what will come next, certainly integrated circuits are not the last stop. Some time in the future, another revolution in electronics will affect people and technology.

KEY WORDS

The reader should be familiar with the following terms in the context in which they were used in the chapter:

Alternating Current

Amp

Amplifier

Base

Battery

Capacitor

Cathode

Chassis

Chip

Circuit

Coil

Collector

Components

Conductor

Cycle

Detector

Diode

Direct Current

Edison Effect

Electricity

Electron

Emitter

Filament

Frequency

Gate

Generator

Grid

Hertz

Inductor

Insulator

Integrated Circuit

Magnetism

Meter

Ohm's Law

Oscillator

Oscilloscope

Parallel

Phase

Plate

Power

Power Supply

Resistor

Schematic Diagram

Semiconductor

Series

Sine Wave

Solid-State

Switch

Systems

Transformer

Transistor

Triode

Tuning

Vacuum Tube

Volt

Volume Control

Watt

Wire

EXERCISES

1. Name two places where direct current is still used today.

2. Draw a basic series circuit using a doorbell, a battery, and a switch.

3. Why is alternating current more difficult to understand than direct current?

4. Where is alternating current used today?

5. What is one major advantage of alternating current over direct current?

6. Name three ways that electricity can be generated.

7. How much air is in a vacuum tube?

8. Name five types of common electronic components.

9. What is an electronic circuit?

10. List three types of electronic circuits.

11. Explain how electronic systems are produced.

12. What are the major advantages of transistors?

13. What has been the impact of integrated circuits on society?

14. Why are electronic circuits important to telecommunications?

3

Computers

The computer has become an integral part of American life, but its operation is still not clearly understood by many people.

This chapter considers some of the basic aspects of computers. It explains how computers are used as standalone devices for general-purpose applications. Also explained are some interrelationships of computers to telecommunications.

FUNDAMENTALS

Computers are very fast logic devices. They are not thinking machines. The computers considered in this chapter do not include attempts at artificial intelligence (AI) or machines that "think".

The term "fast" is often difficult to comprehend when applied to computers. They rely on electricity which works at the speed of light. A

Table 3.1. Numbering Systems _____

Decimal Numbers	Binary Equivalents
0	0
1	01
2	10
3	11
4	100
5	101
6	110
7	111
8	1000
9	1001

great deal can be done in a second in a computer. A second to a computer is literally what years might be to a person, a long period of time to do a great many things.

Computers work in microseconds, one-millionth of a second, and nanoseconds, one-billionth of a second. (In one nanosecond light travels one foot.)

It is the ability to do a great deal in a small instant of time which gives the computer the appearance of being so capable. However, what the computer does is perform logical analysis; it does not use intuition or feelings. Computers do not "think".

The computers being discussed are digital devices. They work with discrete values: zero (0) and one (1). These two values make up the binary numbering system (Table 3.1).

Humans normally work with the decimal numbering system that goes from 0 to 9. Numbers can be added and subtracted in the binary numbering system just as in the decimal system (Table 3.2). However, binary numbers are larger and more cumbersome.

It is often difficult to understand how letters can be represented in terms of zeros and ones. A code is used to represent letters in terms of zeroes and ones, just as the telegraph code uses dots and dashes to represent letters of the alphabet (Table 3.3). Thus, it is possible to have both words and numbers stored in a computer for logical manipulation. Computers have to be told in great detail how to perform logical manipulation. Even simple mistakes in telling a computer what to do can bring it to a halt.

It is *people* who tell computers what to do, and computer errors are usually *people* errors. This may be difficult to fully appreciate, since when computers are working properly they seem so "smart". However,

Table 3.2. Decimal and Binary Calculations

Decimal Addition	Binary Addition
1	01
+ 1	+ 01
2	10

2	10
+ 2	+ 10
4	100

Decimal Subtraction	Binary Subtraction
1	01
− 1	− 01
0	0

4	100
− 2	− 10
2	10

when a computer sends out a bill for $00.00 and then follows up with dunning letters to collect $00.00, it suddenly seems to be not so smart.

It almost sounds like computers are rather dumb, and in a sense that is true. Their operating speeds give them the appearance of more ability than they possess. It is really people who are the "brains" of a computer; they build them and tell them what to do and how to do it.

Computers frustrate people because understanding them is a significant learning experience. One cannot look at a computer, see physical motion, and understand what is going on. Rather, a person has to understand binary numbering systems, very fast speeds, logical processing, etc. to understand computers.

Children often seem to take more quickly to the computer than adults.

Table 3.3. Codes

Character	International Morse Code	Typical Computer Code	
A	. —	1100	0001
B	— . . .	1100	0010
C	— . — .	1100	0011
1	. — — — —	1111	0001
2	. . — — —	1111	0010
3	. . . — —	1111	0011

This is because children have less to forget and are less conscious about new things; they are at a stage in life when everything is new. Also, children are more used to dealing with a lot of failure at learning. Learning how to walk, talk, etc. involves a lot of failing, and these are recent memories to a child.

For adults it is a different story. A great deal of what an adult already knows may interfere with acquiring new knowledge about computers, and adults are much more sensitive about failing. They fear that their reputations are at stake when trying to understand computers. Nevertheless, once they have obtained an understanding of computers, adults have a great ability to figure out what to do with them. Their existing knowledge enables them to determine how computers can best be utilized. Children cannot do this sort of analysis.

Adults can also appreciate the difficulty of introducing new technology into an organization. They know that complex systems often promise more than can realistically be delivered, and that complex systems often fail when they are needed most and people must then take over. So, it is really people who are in charge of computers.

CIRCUITS

Like other electronic devices, computers rely on electronic circuits. An understanding of a few basic computer circuits will be helpful in understanding computers.

One of the most basic circuits is the gate. It is one of the fundamental building blocks of a computer. A gate is an electronic circuit which permits certain specific things to happen on its output depending on what is happening on its input (Figure 3.1).

The input to a gate circuit are the zeroes and ones which are basic to computer operation. However, the gate does not "understand" an abstract symbol like a 0 or 1. So, a 1 can be represented by a flow of electricity for some small instant of time, and a 0 can be represented by the absence of electricity. (The electricity is direct current as discussed in Chapter 2.)

Gates perform the logical decision process which takes place in a computer. The specific logic of a gate circuit can be described in terms of a truth table (Figure 3.1). A truth table shows what the output of a gate will be for a specific combination of inputs.

There are different types of gate circuits, and each has its own unique truth table. Each gate is made up of electronic components. (For simplicity's sake, the components are represented by a simple symbol. This makes it easier to draw schematic diagrams.)

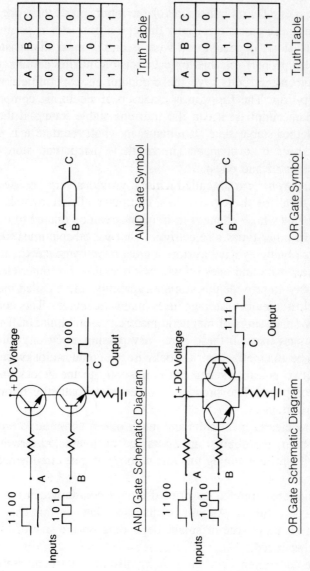

A	B	C
0	0	0
0	1	0
1	0	0
1	1	1

Truth Table

AND Gate Symbol

A	B	C
0	0	0
0	1	1
1	0	1
1	1	1

Truth Table

OR Gate Symbol

AND Gate Schematic Diagram

OR Gate Schematic Diagram

Figure 3.1. Shown above are the schematic diagrams, symbols and truth tables for an AND and OR gate. These are two commonly-used computer gate circuits.

Among the common gates are the AND gate and the OR gate (Figure 3.1). A look at their truth tables reveals some interesting facts. In the AND gate, both inputs must be one (1) to get a one (1) on the output. In the OR gate, a one (1) on either side of the inputs produces a one (1) on the output. In these gates, electricity through a transistor is permitted to flow or not to flow, depending on what is on the input. Transistors act as fast switches to perform this logical decision-making action.

Other electronic circuits give the computer its capabilities. One of them is a flip-flop. The flip-flop is made up of electronic components. Just as the name implies, it can flip into one stable state and then flop back into another stable state. It remains in whatever state it is in until something causes it to change. The result is that it can store digital information (zeroes and ones).

Another electronic circuit called a clock provides very precise timing information to all of the circuits in a computer. This circuit is a very precise oscillator whose changes in frequency can be related to time and is also used in other types of electronics (but for other purposes).

Computers obviously have to store a great quantity of electrical pulses which are the zeroes and ones on which it operates. So, other electronic circuits are used to provide this storage capability, often called memory.

One form of memory storage uses magnetic cores. The cores are actually very small rings of magnetic material resembling small donuts. Small wires pass through these cores. By passing electricity through a core, it can be magnetized in a clockwise or counter-clockwise direction. These two possible states can correspond to the zeroes and ones used in a computer. The process is reversed to read the information stored in core memory.

All of these electronic circuits and many others combine to produce a computer. Often, the circuits are contained on integrated circuits. It is an ideal device for containing the vast number of gate circuits needed in a computer.

The circuits are mounted on printed circuit boards which are in turn mounted inside cabinets. As will be discussed later in this chapter, the cabinets can be very large or small, depending on the size of the computer being produced.

Electronic components and circuits are also used to produce the other devices associated with computers. These include terminals, printers, and other items.

Powering it all is the alternating current discussed in Chapter 2. Via a power supply, this alternating current is converted into direct current for use by the electronic components and circuits of a computer.

HARDWARE

The above-mentioned electronic components and circuits combine to produce computer hardware. Specific hardware components have been considered individually to help simplify the understanding of how a computer system works. However, it should be remembered that computer engineers and technicians have to think about a computer in terms of digital pulses of electricity, the zeroes (0) and ones (1) which are the basis of the computer.

At the heart of the computer is the central processing unit, the CPU (Figure 3.2). This is where the logical analysis is performed. It is like the center ring of a three-ring circus. The other rings are important but the center ring gets more attention.

The CPU consists of two subsystems. One is the control unit and the other is the arithmetic/logical unit. As the name implies, the control unit serves a control function. It receives data in the form of zeroes and ones and provides them to the arithmetic/logical unit as needed for the decision-making actions. It is the ability of the CPU to perform this logical decision-making at such a high rate of speed that makes a computer so useful.

Closely associated with the CPU is the main memory. This is the storage area where data is kept for the CPU. It has very fast access to the data; zeroes and ones are stored here. Magnetic cores are one form of main memory, and there are other forms of storage.

The CPU and main memory combine to form a basic computer system, but inputs and outputs are needed to the system. Logically enough, it is provided in the form of input and output devices.

A punch card reader is one form of input device. It takes punched paper cards on which data has been coded and feeds it into the computer system. On a punched card, the presence or absence of a hole or punch in the paper determines whether a zero or one is being presented to the system. Keyboards can also be used as input devices to the system.

A printer is one example of an output device. Data is printed on paper to provide a hard copy of the results of the computer processing. A display screen or cathode ray tube (CRT) is another example of an output device. A visual display provides information which may not be needed in hard paper copy.

Input and output devices act at a much slower rate of speed than the CPU. Data has to be buffered or temporarily stored for the transfer process to and from input and output devices. This buffering is accomplished by electronic circuits. It permits the CPU to work at a high rate

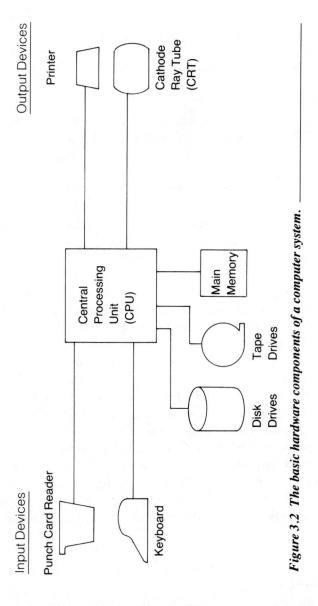

Figure 3.2 The basic hardware components of a computer system.

of speed without having to be concerned about the slow rate of speed of the associated devices.

Additional devices are also typically associated with a total computer system, one of the main ones being auxiliary storage devices. While main memory is fast, it is also a relatively expensive form of memory or storage. The auxiliary storage devices offer a less expensive alternative for large amounts of data. Tape and disk drives are the most widely-used forms of auxiliary storage.

A tape drive uses magnetic tape to store data as magnetic spots. The spots are the zeroes and ones which a computer uses. Information on magnetic tape is stored sequentially on tape, and a great deal of data can be stored on a reel of tape. To access the data, the tape must be read sequentially. If the data needed is at the end of the reel, the access process can be rather slow.

Data is stored on disk drives in the form of magnetic spots corresponding to zeroes and ones. However, unlike tape drive, data on the disk drive can be accessed directly. This is similar to placing the needle of a record player directly on any song on a record. Thus, the access time of a disk drive is much faster than the access time of a tape drive.

Auxiliary storage devices also operate at a much slower speed than the CPU. So, data to and from them is buffered to improve the efficiency of the overall computer system.

Auxiliary storage devices can also be used as input and output devices. Data from them can be inputed to the computer for processing and the output can be returned to them for storage. This is a common occurrence in large and medium-sized computer operations.

Auxiliary storage devices are made up of electronic and electro-mechanical components, circuits and systems. Electricity makes them operate. They come in all sizes, from the very large to the very small. The fact that there is mechanical motion associated with them often makes them seem more real than the CPU. All they do, though, is follow the laws of electricity and electronics.

All of the hardware components of a computer work together to produce a total computer system. Electrical pulses in the form of zeroes and ones flow through each of the individual pieces of hardware and between hardware components to produce an amazingly complex but effective system.

SOFTWARE

It takes more than hardware to make a computer work. It also takes software, computer programs, to make it functional. Software is sometimes difficult for people to understand; it is something like the music on a record. A stereo system and a record are hardware, but it is the music on the record which makes the system meaningful. In the same manner, software makes a computer meaningful.

Computer programs—software—are the instructions that tell the computer hardware what to do. Programs become the zeroes and ones in the computer. There are various programming languages which programmers use to write computer programs (Table 3.4).

In the early days of computers, the programs were actually written in zeroes and ones. This is called machine language. Writing programs in this manner is a tremendously difficult task. The human mind has great difficulty in dealing with vast quantities of zeroes and ones.

So, assembler language was developed. It uses symbols which resemble shorthand symbols. This was a big step forward over using zeroes and ones. The human mind deals better with letters of the alphabet and words.

To further improve the efficiency of programmers, higher level computer languages have been developed. Among the better known ones are BASIC, COBOL and FORTRAN. However, there are also many other computer languages.

BASIC (Beginner's All-purpose Symbolic Instruction Code) was developed by Dr. John Kemeny with the assistance of Dr. Thomas Kurtz and others at Dartmouth College. COBOL (COmmon Business Oriented Language) was developed by a committee. FORTRAN (FORmula TRANslation) was developed by John Backus and others at IBM.

BASIC is widely used on personal computers, COBOL is used in

Table 3.4. Computer Programming Languages _____

(Partial listing)

Name	Illustration
Machine	01011010
Assembler	L 2,A
BASIC	GOTO 100
COBOL	READ CARD-FILE
FORTRAN	READ (6,12) RADIUS

BASIC = Beginner's All-purpose Symbolic Instruction Code

COBOL = COmmon Business Oriented Language

FORTRAN = FORmula TRANslation

business applications, and FORTRAN is used in engineering and scientific work. Each language has its advantages and limitations.

In machine and assembler programming, each line of computer code or instruction equates to a specific action in the computer. A knowledge of computer hardware is needed to program in these languages. In the higher level languages, a line of code or an instruction may automatically be converted by the computer into multiple instructions. Such languages do not require the hardware knowledge of machine and assembler programming. They are much more problem-oriented and designed to be easier to use by a wide range of programmers.

There are programs in a computer that convert the programs written in BASIC, COBOL, etc. into electrical pulses—zeroes and ones. These programs are called compilers. The programs written in BASIC, FORTRAN, etc. are often called application programs because they are designed for specific applications.

There are other computer programs called operating systems. They control the operation of the other programs within the computer. They are internal "traffic managers". The operating system programs can control access to input and output devices, auxiliary storage, etc. Operating system programs help to simplify the duties of the programmers who are writing the application programs.

Before writing a computer program, a flowchart is developed by the programmer. It shows all of the steps and actions to be accomplished by the program, and is similar to preparing an outline before writing a report. The flowchart helps to simplify the programming process.

The preparation of a program takes place one step at a time in a flowchart. Each computer language has its own rules, just as English has rules of grammar. However, computers have to be told in exact and total detail every step that is to be taken and what to do when problems (bugs) arise. Bugs are mistakes, flaws, and errors. Typically, they are found in computer programs, although they also occur in computer hardware. Sometimes, bugs in computer programs are not discovered until long after the program has been used, and they are then often modified to correct the bugs. Unfortunately, the changes or modifications can introduce new bugs. The task of correction can be never-ending with large programs.

A small program can be written by one programmer. Large programs are written by teams of programmers, each team working on a separate part.

Operating system programs, application programs, compilers, etc. are typically developed by vendors for use by many different organizations.

This helps to reduce programming costs. Such prepackaged application programs, though, may not meet the needs of every organization, and so specialized programs may have to be developed by the using organization.

SIZE

Computer systems can be categorized as large, medium, small or personal, and very small. There are overlaps between these categories.

Large computer systems are the oldest and are still widely used today. They are physically large and occupy their own rooms which have raised floors, special power, special air-conditioning, etc. The hardware components sit in large cabinets on the computer room floor. There is a cabinet for the central processor (CPU), a cabinet for the main memory, and cabinets for the auxiliary storage devices, the disks, and the tape drives. The input and output devices may be in the same room as the cabinets or in a separate room. (Printers can be noisy devices, and a large number of them are often best kept in a separate room. This also helps to reduce the number of personnel who need access to the main computer area.)

Medium-sized systems are often found in organizations which do not need the power of a large system but need more than the power of a small or personal computer. Such systems often have their own room, but there are fewer cabinets for auxiliary storage. Also, the CPU cabinet and other equipment may be physically smaller than what is found in a large system.

Large and medium-sized systems are normally designed to perform multiple tasks at the same time. This makes them well-suited to the needs of business organizations and multiple users.

Small, personal, and microprocessor computers are a recent addition to the computer family. These are the desktop computers which are a product of integrated circuit technology. These systems sometimes have the central processor, main memory, auxiliary storage, and input and output devices all in one cabinet. Typically, there is a typewriter-style keyboard to be used for input and a cathode ray tube and/or printer for output. The auxiliary storage device is normally one or more disk drives.

In personal computers, the main memory is called RAM (Random Access Memory). It is used for the temporary storage of data being processed by the CPU. Another type of memory, ROM (Read Only Memory), is permanently stored. ROM data can be read and used but cannot be altered.

Computer programs are typically entered into the system via a disk drive. Data to be processed can be entered via the keyboard and the results can be displayed on a CRT or printed in hard copy on a printer. Personal computers are normally designed to perform one task at a time.

Users of small or personal computers are discovering what operators of larger systems have known for years—computers are not perfect. For instance, static electricity generated by walking across a carpet can cause computer problems. Large amounts of data can be accidentally lost, so the importance of having back-up copies of data becomes self-evident.

Learning to operate a personal computer can be a challenge. Instruction manuals are often long, complex and difficult to relate to the task at hand. Users are often unprepared for the amount of time it takes to learn how to operate a personal computer.

Very small computers are typically used inside of other equipment or systems for specific functions. Such systems are not designed to perform general-purpose activities. A very small computer can be installed in a data terminal device to give it some specialized but limited data processing capability, such as editing data before it is sent to a computer for complex processing. Other specialized computers are often used in telecommunications equipment and will be described later in this chapter. They are not designed to be used for general data processing activities.

APPLICATIONS

An understanding of computer applications will help to provide a clear understanding of what computers can do, why they seem so powerful, and why it is so easy to forget that they are really just fast logic devices (Table 3.5).

One of the oldest applications for computers is called batch processing and is still widely used today. In this type of application, the data to be processed is physically brought to the computer. A specific application is processed all at the same time in a batch. For example, payroll cards may be processed in a batch to produce payroll checks and payroll reports.

Batch processing is similar to a manufacturing plant where the customer brings raw material to the plant and later returns to pick up the finished product. Jobs are scheduled, but some delays can be tolerated.

With batch processing, users have only indirect access to the computer. The operators, schedulers, etc. are the interfaces to the computer. For many types of data processing, this is a very satisfactory

Table 3.5. Computer Applications _____

Batch Processing

Payroll
Accounts Receivable
Billing Statements

Via Telecommunications

Reservations
Order Entry
Rate Quotations

operation, but for other types of data processing more direct access to a large computer system is needed.

Users might have direct access to a system via a terminal on their desks. Such access is often called time-sharing. This is possible because people work at much slower speeds than a large computer system which may have hundreds of local terminals accessing it at the same time.

This direct access means that a user can enter data and see the results of the computer processing displayed on a screen in a matter of seconds. It did not take long for people to understand the advantage of being able to extend the power of large computers beyond the buildings in which they are located. Chapter 5 discusses the technical aspects of remotely communicating with a computer.

An early use for remotely accessing a large computer was time-sharing. Terminals might be hundreds or thousands of miles from the computer, and each user can still use his terminal for specific purposes.

Many organizations have realized that remotely-accessed large computers can be used for specific dedicated tasks. The airlines were among the early users of such systems. Via telecommunications, they could access a central computer to schedule airline passengers and to sell tickets. These remote terminals at airports, ticket offices, etc. brought a new level of sophistication to the operation of airlines.

Banks and insurance companies have also made tremendous use of remotely-accessed computers. In the past, large amounts of data would have to be brought to the central computer for processing. Time delays were often significant in processing data and returning it to the originators. The installation of remote terminals in branch offices now permits bank tellers to immediately determine the status of customer accounts. Bank loan officers can instantly review a customer's account when discussing a loan application.

Insurance personnel can take a terminal to a customer's home and remotely enter data to get instant rate quotes. This means that sales can often be closed on the spot. This has helped to increase the productivity of the insurance industry.

Industrial companies also use remote access. Order entry is an illustration of one widely-used application. In the past, orders from field offices were typically mailed to distribution centers for processing and shipment to customers. Today, remote terminals and telecommunications enable field sales offices to first check on the availability of an item. The order can then be entered to the computer. In turn, the computer routes the order to the proper distribution center for processing and shipment. The field office can check on the status of the order to know when it was shipped.

Many individuals have personal computers in their homes that can be used as terminal devices to remotely access larger computers via telecommunications networks. This is often done to access large data bases of information stored in the larger computers. Individuals can use this ability for both personal and business activities.

ROLE IN TELECOMMUNICATIONS

The early role of telecommunications was to provide services to computers. Now, computers are providing many services to the field of telecommunications (Table 3.6). This has brought about a revolution in telecommunications.

Computers have become part of today's telephone networks. Computers are part of the switching systems found in telephone company central offices and the telephone systems used in business. Computers can analyze telephone numbers to determine how the call can best be routed, and select alternate routes in case of difficulties. Computers can remember if a called number is busy and can continue calling it indefinitely. When the call is completed, the originating party can be automatically called back for his or her call.

Computers can keep track of long distance telephone calls in a business organization's telephone system. Calls can be routed over the

Table 3.6. Computers in Telecommunications _____

Telephone Systems
Data Communications Equipment
Data Communication Networks
Automobile Telephones
Radio and TV Broadcasting

least expensive lines and a record can be kept of each call for the purpose of cost allocation.

The computers built into telephone systems are special-purpose computers designed for the specific application of controlling telephone calls. However, they work on the same principles as general-purpose computers.

The addition of computers to telephone systems has affected personnel in the telephone industry. Traditionally, the industry relied on electro-mechanical technology, switches and relays that used electricity and magnetism. The introduction of computers has meant that engineers and technicians must now be knowledgeable in computer technology. For the people in the industry, this has required significant learning experiences.

The car telephone based on cellular technology will be described in Chapter 6. This technology is based on computer control. The fast logic of the computer enables such systems to operate effectively. Previously, without computers, the availability of telephone service from automobiles was limited to only a few subscribers. Today, in major cities, a telephone in a car is available to anyone who wants the service.

Computer technology enables complex data communications activities to be monitored and controlled. The systems can diagnose themselves and report problems to the operators of the system. The computer can keep track of trends and can project possible failures which might occur.

Since data communications systems are frequently critical to an organization, their effective management and operation is of the highest importance. As systems go from hundreds to thousands of remote computer terminals, it will take computer technology to keep such systems performing at maximum efficiency. Such systems will still need human operators, but they will not have to monitor vast amounts of data. Rather, the computer can monitor the data and advise the operators regarding problems which need to be investigated.

New data communications networks are being developed based on computer technology. (They will be discussed in detail in Chapter 8.) Such networks are designed only for computer communications and data communications. They do not handle voice telephone calls. These networks use special computers as the switches to route data communications traffic. Again, the fast logic power of the computer makes this specialized application possible.

Computers have also become widely used in the radio and TV broadcasting industry. Obviously, they can be used for routine data processing activities such as payroll and report generation, and also have many specialized applications. A radio station can be automated by a computer. The music, commercials, etc. can be automatically selected and played from tapes prepared in advance. Live announcers are not needed at all. Rather, operator personnel monitor the system for any possible failure which the system cannot automatically correct.

Specialized computer systems can also be used to automatically monitor and control radio and TV transmitter systems. These systems are often remotely located from the studio in which the programs originate. Rather than having an operator at the transmitter site, a computer system can automatically monitor the operation of the transmitter and advise operator personnel at the studio of any problems. In the case of major problems, repair personnel can be dispatched to the transmitter site.

KEY WORDS

The reader should be familiar with the following terms in the context in which they were used in this chapter:

AND Gate

Application Programs

Arithmetic/Logic Unit

Assembler

Auxiliary Storage

BASIC

Batch Processing

Binary

Buffer

Bug

Circuit

Clock

COBOL

Code

Compiler

Control Unit

CPU

CRT

Digital

Disk Drive

Flip-Flop

Flowchart

FORTRAN

Gate

Hardware

Input Device

Keyboard

Logic

Machine Language

Magnetic Cores

Main Memory

Microsecond

Nanosecond

One

Operating System

OR Gate

Output Device

Program

Punch Card

Printer

RAM

ROM

Software

Tape Drive

Terminal

Time-Sharing

Truth Table

Zero

EXERCISES

1. How fast can a computer operate?

2. What are the two quantities that a computer works with?

3. Why are codes used in computers?

4. Explain the difference between an AND gate and an OR gate.

5. Does a truth table always tell the truth?

6. Draw a diagram showing the main hardware components of a computer system.

7. Why are auxiliary storage devices needed?

8. What is the purpose of computer programs?

9. Why are computer programs not perfect?

10. What has made possible the development of personal computers?

11. Why do large computers exist?

12. Explain the difference between batch processing and applications which use telecommunications.

13. Name three areas in telecommunications that have been affected by computers.

4

Telephone Systems

THE TELEPHONE
THE CENTRAL OFFICE
SWITCHING
SWITCHING EQUIPMENT
TRANSMISSION
PRIVATE TELEPHONE SYSTEMS
ANALOG VERSUS DIGITAL
KEY WORDS
EXERCISES

The telephone system has been in existence for so many years that it is simply taken for granted. People seldom stop to think about what it takes to provide telephone service.

This chapter covers the basic technical components of the telephone system and of local telephone service. Long distance communications will be covered in Chapter 8.

THE TELEPHONE

The telephone system is often thought about in terms of the telephone set or instrument found on almost every business desk and in most homes in the U.S. However, most people have never stopped to consider how a telephone functions or to what it is connected.

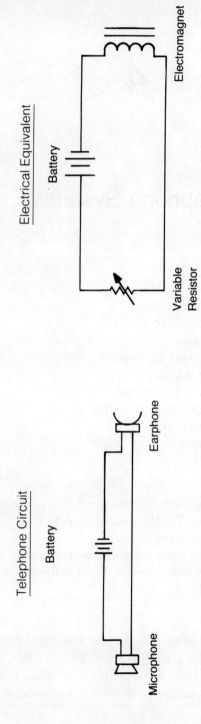

Figure 4.1. A simple telephone circuit and its electrical equivalent. The drawing on the left shows a simple telephone circuit consisting of a microphone, earphone and battery. The drawing on the right shows that the microphone appears as a variable resistor and the earphone appears as an electromagnet.

Figure 4.1 shows a simple telephone circuit that consists of a carbon microphone, a battery, and an electro-mechanical earphone. This circuit is capable of transmitting human speech over wires. The battery supplies the direct current voltage for the circuit. The microphone consists of a diaphragm placed on top of carbon granules. The diaphragm and granules are mounted in a small case. When someone speaks into the microphone, the air vibrations cause the diaphragm to vibrate. This causes the electrical resistance of the carbon granules to vary, which in turn causes variations in the flow of the direct current.

The earphone consists of a diaphragm placed on top of a coil of wire wrapped around a permanent magnet. The flow of electricity through the coil creates an electromagnet. As the flow of electricity varies in response to human speech at the microphone, the strength of the magnetic field in the earphone also varies. This causes the diaphragm in the earphone to vibrate. These vibrations cause vibrations in the air which are received by the human ear as sounds and human speech.

Thus, through a rather simple process, human speech can be transmitted over wires. As you can see, the telephone is based on a rather simple technology.

The introduction of the dial to the telephone was a big step forward in the telephone industry. It was part of the automation of the telephone industry. Today, it provides a caller access to a gigantic local and long distance telephone network.

A rotary dial takes the dialed digits and transforms them into dial pulses, which is electrical information that the local telephone company central office can use. The rotary dial makes and breaks the direct current connection from the central office in response to the number of digits being dialed (Figure 4.2).

When a number pad is used in place of a rotary dial, a different type of dialing operation takes place. A pad is used to generate tones which reflect the number being called. When tones are sent over the telephone circuit, it is similar to a person whistling over the circuit; the direct current is not broken to create dial pulses. A pad permits the user to enter the called number much more rapidly than the rotary dial.

A feature on every telephone set that is often overlooked is the switch hook. When a caller lifts the handset, he goes off-hook to tell the central office that a call is to be made. When the handset is hung up, the switch hook is reactivated to tell the central office that the call is completed. The switch hook provides a basic automatic signalling service to the central office. In the original telephone sets, the switch hook resembled a very large hook, and thus the term came into existence.

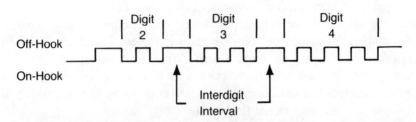

Figure 4.2. Shown are the rotary dial pulses for the number 234. The rotary dial on the telephone makes and breaks the direct current electricity from the central office.

When a caller goes off-hook, a dial tone is provided by the central office. The dial tone tells the calling party that the central office is ready to receive the called telephone number. After this number has been entered, a ringing tone is heard. It tells the caller that the called number is being rung. If the called number is busy, the calling party hears a busy tone instead of a ringing tone.

The telephone is connected to the local telephone company central office via a pair of copper wires. The wires from a home are connected to a telephone pole where they join with other wires in a cable, which is multiple pairs of wires contained in one covering.

THE CENTRAL OFFICE

The telephone set is only the tip of a vast iceberg. The telephone company central office is the next part of this iceberg. The central office is the building that houses equipment used to switch telephone calls. In a small town, one building can serve everyone. In large cities, the central office might be in a large building, and there may be more buildings within the city.

The central office is within a few miles of the customers served by the office. Central offices are provided by the local telephone company in each city and town. Each local telephone company is responsible for the central offices and the local telephone service.

A central office can be divided into main sections (Figure 4.3). The wires which enter the central office terminate on a distribution frame which serves as a cross-connect point. The equipment located within the central office also terminates on the distribution frame. Wires (jumpers) go between termination points on the frame to establish the electrical

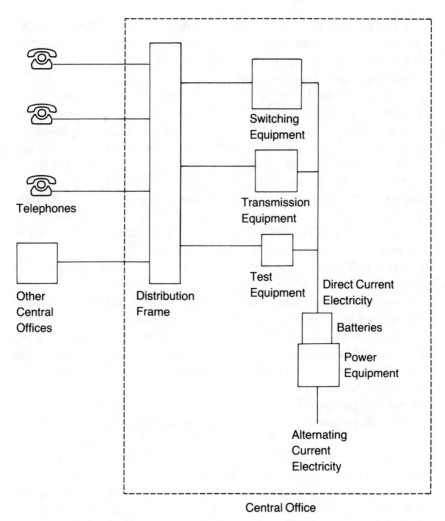

Figure 4.3. A telephone central office with its main sections. _____

connections between the external wires and the equipment within the central office.

In large offices, employees are assigned to work on the frame. When a new telephone is assigned to a customer, the telephone wires coming from the telephone have to be cross-connected to the proper location on the switching equipment which is the heart of the central office. (The actual equipment will be described later in this chapter.) The switching equipment sets up the connection between the caller and the called party.

In large central offices, switching equipment typically handles 10,000 customers. Cities with hundreds of thousands of people have multiple sets of switching equipment; a small town with only a few thousand people might have only one switch.

Another area in the office contains transmission equipment. This is electronic equipment designed to amplify signals which go to other central offices. (Transmission equipment will be described later in this chapter.)

There is often an area set aside for test equipment which is designed to perform tests on the wires which leave the building and go to the telephone sets and other central offices. With thousands of wires entering and leaving the central office, it is important for the central office personnel to be able to rapidly isolate problems on these wires. The test personnel talk with installation and repair personnel outside of the central office and also talk with other repair personnel who work within the office.

A separate area of equipment converts alternating current to the direct current used by telephone equipment. Normally, the direct current has a battery back-up. If the alternating current from the power company fails, the batteries continue to supply power to the central office. This means that telephones can remain in operation even when lights go out at home or work.

Central office equipment represents a significant capital expense. It is designed to remain in service for many years. This also helps to reduce maintenance costs and, ultimately, the cost of providing service.

As cities expand into the suburbs, new central offices have to be built. It is often difficult to predict such growth and to keep up with customer demand. Telephone company personnel monitor building and construction permits, and growth projections for a given area are carefully considered. The idea is to have the central office available when needed but not too far ahead of time.

It takes relatively few people to operate a central office; the equipment is highly automatic. Even during strikes, management personnel are able to keep central office equipment operational. Some central offices are even unattended. They are monitored remotely and repair personnel are dispatched as needed. The new generation of computer-controlled switching systems is well-suited to remote monitoring.

Countries outside of the U.S. also utilize the central office concept. Different types of equipment supplied by different vendors may be used, but the same general principles of organization and layout are followed.

In developing countries, it is often difficult for the local telephone company to keep up with the demand for service. A telephone might be a luxury item, and it might take months or years to get one. Also, the company may have difficulty keeping up with the demands of those who do have telephones.

SWITCHING

In the early days of the telephone industry, wires were strung directly from one subscriber to another. This was fine for people who needed to constantly talk to each other. However, to provide many subscribers access to each other, it would be inefficient to directly connect them all together (Figure 4.4), and so switching came into existence.

Under the switching concept, users are connected to a central switch (Figure 4.5). It serves as a control point to permit subscribers to easily call anyone. This basic concept has been fundamental to the development of the telephone system.

The first switches were manual switchboards. (They will be discussed

WITHOUT SWITCHING

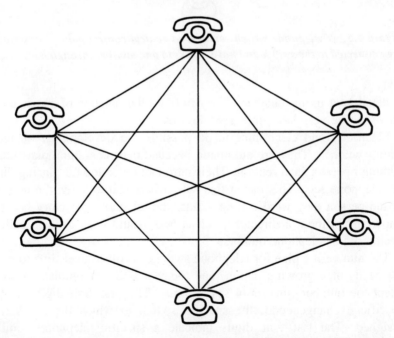

Figure 4.4. A telephone system without switching. Every subscriber has to be wired directly to every other subscriber.

WITH SWITCHING

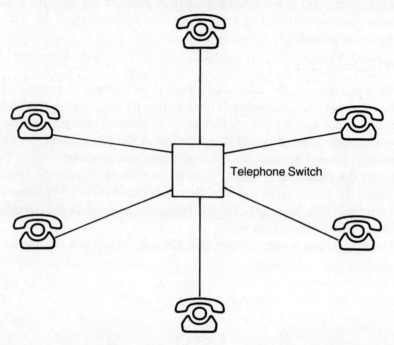

Figure 4.5. A telephone switch serves as a central control point. Subscribers are connected to the switch and have access to one another through it. _____

in detail later in this chapter.) They fulfilled the function of a switch but proved to be very labor-intensive devices.

Electricity and electronics made possible the development of automatic switches. They are automatic because their operation takes place without operator intervention. Their introduction called for placing dials on telephone sets. This meant that subscribers had to know the number of the person they were calling. Thus, the telephone directory became important; without a directory, subscribers would have to keep calling operators for telephone numbers.

The numbering plan for telephone switches evolved over time to meet the needs of a growing nation, and today it is quite complex. A local telephone number consists of seven digits. The first three digits are the specific exchange code, the specific switch to which the number is assigned. The last four digits indicate a specific telephone number within the switch. The exchange code permits subscribers with different exchange codes to have the same last four digits in a given telephone number. In most large cities there are multiple exchange codes to handle all of the subscribers. However, in a small town there might be only one code.

Area codes evolved in the U.S. to divide the country into different sections so that the same exchange codes could be used within different area codes. States that are not heavily populated might have only one area code. However, many states have multiple area codes. As the population within a state continues to expand, it is often necessary to add new area codes.

The world is divided into codes for different countries. This makes possible the direct dialing of telephone calls from the U.S. to a great many foreign countries.

In the U.S., most long distance telephone calls are preceded by the digit 1. This is to advise the central office that what follows is a long distance call. The central office can then immediately route the call to a long distance telephone switch. So, a small burden has been placed on the subscribers to improve the overall efficiency of the system.

Within a city, the various central offices are interconnected by wires and cables. There is also a special category of telephone switch which can be used to connect central offices. It is called a tandem switch (Figure 4.6). This helps to greatly simplify the interconnection of local central offices with each other.

Central office equipment was predicated on the calling patterns of subscribers. Statistics were developed for the length of a typical telephone call, how many people would make calls at any given time, etc. Traffic engineers developed these figures. They are concerned, for instance, with predicting how much switching equipment should be installed in a new central office.

Over the years traffic analysis and predictions have become reliable. This has helped to insure that the optimal equipment is installed but excess equipment is not installed. Unnecessary equipment is only wasted money sitting in a central office.

SWITCHING EQUIPMENT

The earliest switching equipment was the manual switchboard where operators completed every call. These boards had small holes called jacks, one for each subscriber. A light by the jack or an audio signal would tell the operator that a subscriber had gone off-hook and wanted to make a call. The operator would then place one end of a pair of cords into the jack, and so could talk to the calling party. After determining who the calling party wanted to talk to, the operator would plug the

TANDEM SWITCHING

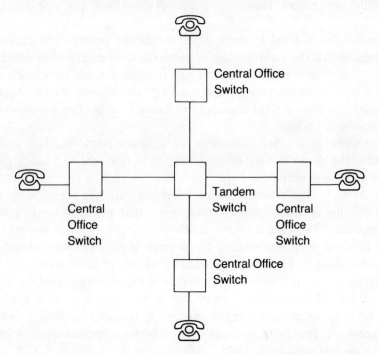

Figure 4.6. A tandem switch can be used to interconnect central office switches. This helps to simplify the interconnection of central offices. ____

other end of the cord pair into the jack for the called party. When the called party answered, the operator would drop out of the call.

Now, Almon Brown Strowger, an undertaker, was concerned that the local operator was giving his competitors his share of the undertaking business. So, he developed a telephone switch that did not need a switchboard operator. This is called a step-by-step switch, or a Strowger switch. It started the telephone central office on the way to automatic operation. However, it also required that dials be placed on telephones. The dial controlled the automatic switch.

The step-by-step switch was the basis for a switching system that could automatically switch telephone calls with multiple digits. It is called a progressive system since each dialed digit takes the call progressively further through the system. When the last digit is dialed, the call is at the called telephone.

Figure 4.7 shows a simple step-by-step switching system. The line finder switch determines when the called party goes off-hook. This

STEP-BY-STEP SWITCHING

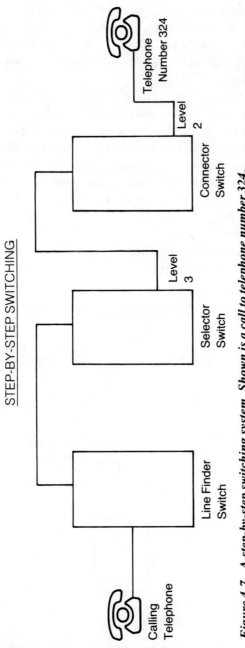

Figure 4.7. A step-by-step switching system. Shown is a call to telephone number 324.

switch is connected to a selector switch that selects the first digit of the dialed number. For example, in a small system, if the called number is 324, when the digit 3 is dialed, the selector switch steps up to the third level which is wired to a connector switch. When the digit 2 is dialed, the connector switch steps up to level 2. When the digit 4 is dialed, the connector switch steps across to position 4 on the switch and telephone number 324 is rung.

The term "step-by-step" comes from the stepping action of the switch. Even a small switching system can have many individual switches all moving at the same time and the result can be a great deal of noise. However, such systems are still in use today around the world.

There are disadvantages to step-by-step systems. One of the major ones is that a great number of switches are needed in a system and they remain in use during each call. Also, these systems take up a great deal of physical space in a central office, and the stepping action subjects them to a great deal of wear.

So, another generation of switching equipment was needed. It came in the form of common control switching equipment (Figure 4.8).

COMMON CONTROL SWITCHING

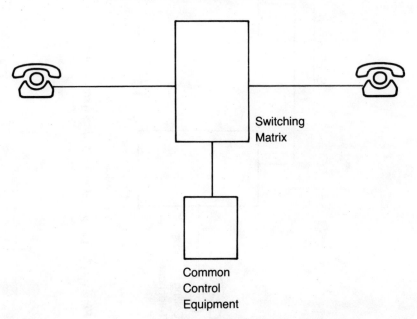

Switching Matrix

Common Control Equipment

Figure 4.8. The common control equipment sets up the calling path through the switching matrix.

The crossbar system was one of the original common control switching systems. These were electro-mechanical in nature. The switching matrix established the connections for each call. It was similar to a railroad switching yard where trains on various tracks are switched to other tracks.

Common control systems using crossbar switches could be made much smaller than comparable step-by-step systems. In addition, their operation was less subject to mechanical wear.

The term "common control" refers to common equipment which detects when the calling party goes off-hook. This equipment collects the dialed digits and sets up the calling path through the crossbar switch. This is similar to a person in a railroad switching yard reading all of the routing information for a specific train and then throwing all of the switches to get the train on the proper track and out of the yard.

The invention of the computer has made possible a new generation of central office switches. These switches use computers to provide the common control functions of setting up each call.

Computer-controlled switches use a switching matrix. Originally, they used electronic components in place of the electro-mechanical matrices which had been utilized. This resulted in a more efficient system which was less subject to mechanical wear.

Computer-controlled switches are normally installed in new central offices. These switches offer many features and flexibility. By changing the computer program which controls their operation, new features and services can easily be added to the system.

The most recent development in computer-controlled switches has been the introduction of digital switches. This means that analog speech is converted into digital form before it is switched by the system. Such systems are thus very suitable for switching digital computer communications.

TRANSMISSION

If the switch is the heart of the central office, the transmission facilities are the arteries and veins through which calls flow to and from the central office.

Wire is the most basic transmission medium for telephone communications. Normally, it is a pair of two copper wires, each having insulating material around it. When a large number of wires are needed, they are combined into a sheath to produce a cable. Wires and cables can be buried in the ground or erected on telephone poles.

In recent years, buried cables have become common. They are much less likely to be damaged by ice, falling telephone poles, etc. Rather than burying them in the ground, they are usually run in conduits under city streets.

To further reduce the damage to cables by water, the cables are often made into sealed systems into which dry air or nitrogen is pumped. The entire system is kept under pressure. This makes it difficult for water and other detrimental matter to enter the cable and affect its performance.

The wires between the telephone set and the central office provide a path for direct current. It is direct current that is sent from the central office to the telephone set. This direct current varies in direct response to the speech of the person talking into a telephone.

A ringing current is sent from the central office over the wires to ring telephone sets. This current is an alternating current voltage that is present only during the ringing cycle. Here, both alternating and direct current continue to coexist.

The wires and cables from the central office carry human speech in the range of approximately 300 to 3,000 Hz. This is normally adequate for a telephone conversation. By way of contrast, a stereo record system reproduces frequencies as high as 20,000 Hz.

Amplification equipment is needed to maintain the strength of the telephone conversations between central offices. Also, to obtain a maximum utilization of the wires and cables between central offices, multiplexing equipment is often used. This equipment enables multiple telephone conversations to go over the same pair of wires.

There are two main types of multiplexing equipment. The older type uses frequency division multiplexing which stacks telephone conversations and passes them over the same pair of wires (Figure 4.9). This is possible because a pair of wires can handle a wider range of frequencies than the 300 to 3,000 Hz of a typical call. This stacking technique is accomplished by equipment which uses electronic circuits. The equipment converts each telephone conversation to a higher frequency range for transmission, and equipment at the distant end converts the signals back to their basic frequency range.

A more recent approach is to use a newer technique called time division multiplexing (Figure 4.10). This approach utilizes a sampling technique for each call. The sampling takes place thousands of times per second. By sampling each call at a rapid rate, it is possible to obtain what is being said without having to transmit the entire call. This is possible because of the rapid sampling rate. Many conversations can thus be carried over the same pair of wires.

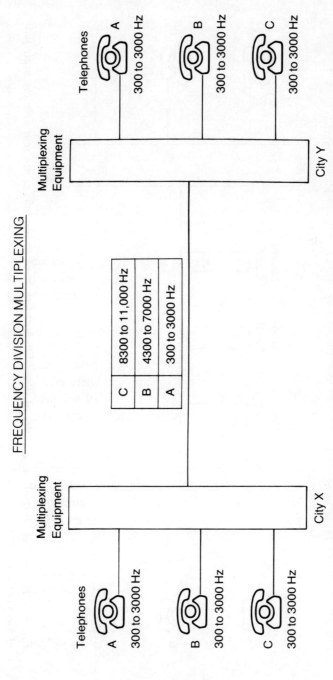

FREQUENCY DIVISION MULTIPLEXING

Figure 4.9. *In this illustration, three telephone conversations are sent over the same pair of wires at the same time through a process of frequency conversion and stacking.*

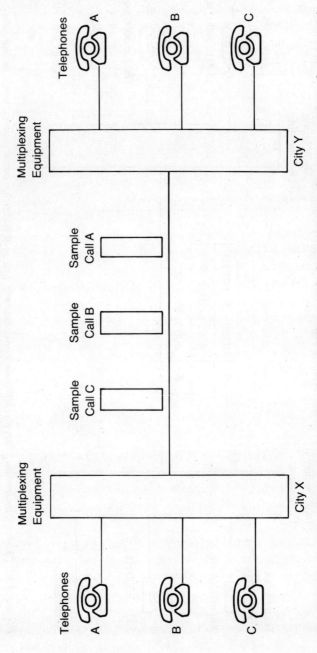

Figure 4.10. In this illustration, samples of three different telephone conversations are sent over the same pair of wires at a rapid rate.

Multiplexing equipment is not inexpensive. It is used where there is a large volume of telephone calls going between two central offices which are a significant distance from each other. The cost of the multiplexing equipment is offset by reductions in the need for expensive wires and cables between the central offices.

PRIVATE TELEPHONE SYSTEMS

Private telephone systems are found in many businesses. One type— the private branch exchange (PBX)—is a telephone switch. It is a miniature central office designed to serve only one customer.

When a PBX is installed, the telephones in a business are connected directly to it. The PBX in turn is connected to the local telephone company central office (Figure 4.11). The number of lines to the central office is usually much less than the number of telephone sets because everyone will not need to call the central office at the same time.

The logic behind a PBX is that users have a community of interest with each other. Rather than have them call through a central office to talk, they can just call through the PBX.

Within a PBX system, the telephone sets typically have only a two-, three- or four-digit number. To make a call thus requires dialing only two, three or four digits. To call outside the PBX to the central office, the caller must first dial the digit 9 and then hears a second dial tone which comes directly from the local central office.

Incoming calls to the PBX are also via wires (lines) from the central office. These calls are answered by the PBX operator who can route them to the proper PBX telephone. In some PBX systems, it is also possible for callers to call directly to a PBX telephone, bypassing the PBX operator.

The first private switches used in business organizations were manual switchboards. They were a smaller version of the manual switchboards used in central offices. A business had to have a switchboard operator to handle calls within the organization and calls to and from the central office.

When automatic switching equipment was developed, PBXs came into existence. The first PBX systems were based on the step-by-step switch, required their own room, were very noisy but provided automatic operation. Actually, these systems were quite flexible and typically had battery back-up, just like central office switches.

The introduction of common control switching systems in the central offices was eventually transferred to PBX systems. Common control

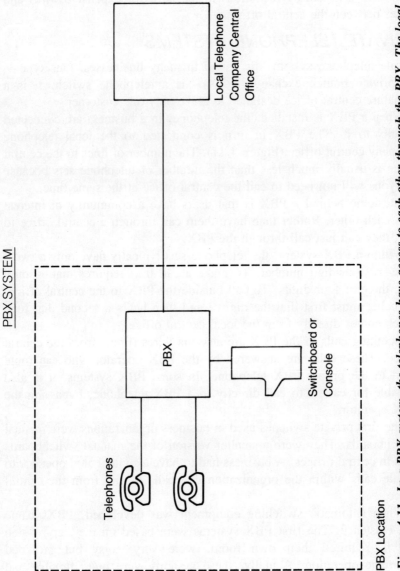

Figure 4.11. In a PBX system, the telephones have access to each other through the PBX. The local central office can also be accessed via the PBX.

PBXs using electro-mechanical crossbar switches could be smaller in size than a step-by-step system and offered more features.

The next step in the PBX evolution was the replacement of the electro-mechanical switching matrix with a matrix using electronic components. This further helped to improve the reliability of the system.

Continuing to follow central office evolution, computer-controlled PBXs came into existence. They provided the PBX with the sophisticated capability that only a computer can provide. A computer-controlled PBX can automatically redial busy numbers and call the calling party back when the call can be completed. Users can dial-in special codes to have their calls rerouted to other telephones. Long distance calls can be queued for access to special long distance lines, the calling party being automatically called back when a line is available. The list of features is long and continues to grow.

The early PBXs were analog systems. Gradually, PBXs with a digital switching matrix came into existence. This follows the trend in central office switching equipment. This move to a digital switching capability in PBXs is in response to the growing need for computer and data communications.

A business which needs only a few telephones—approximately 40 or less—might find a PBX too large for its needs. A key telephone system (KTS) is often used by these smaller organizations (Figure 4.12).

In a key telephone system, local central office lines are directly terminated on each telephone. Incoming calls can be answered by any telephone. To make outgoing calls, a user directly accesses any central office line. An intercommunications line permits users to call one another without going through the central office. A special hold feature enables calls to be held without the calling party hearing background noise.

It is possible for organizations to have in effect a private telephone system by dedicating part of the central office switch to the organization (Figure 4.13). Such systems were called Centrex, but today they have often been renamed for marketing reasons.

With this type of service, each telephone is connected directly to the central office switch. In addition, an operator's console is connected to the dedicated portion of the switch. Normally, the organization is reasonably close to the switch, which minimizes the length of the cable needed for the telephones and the console. Incoming calls are dialed directly to each telephone within the organization, but the operator can

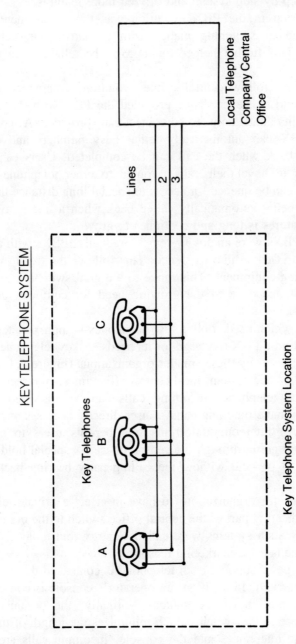

Figure 4.12. In this system, the central office lines terminate directly on each telephone.

CENTREX TELEPHONE SYSTEM

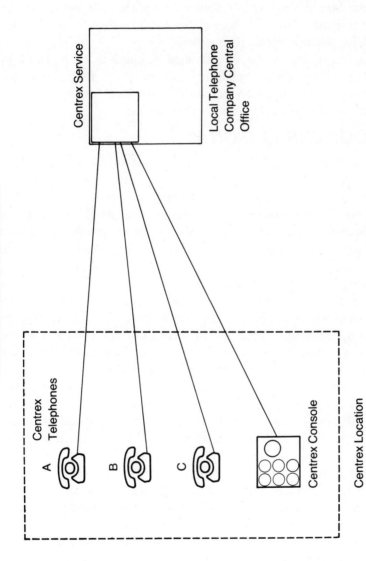

Figure 4.13. In a Centrex system, each telephone is connected directly to the dedicated portion of the switch in the local central office. The attendant's console is also connected directly to the dedicated portion.

reroute incoming calls to the console to any of the telephones in the system.

Calls from one telephone to another within the organization are routed through the dedicated portion of the switch. An exchange code —the first three digits—is not needed. To place calls outside of the dedicated portion of the switch, a caller dials the digit 9 and then the local or long distance telephone number.

This dedicated type of service seemed destined to be replaced by computer-controlled PBXs, but the divestiture of the Bell System has sparked a rebirth of interest on the part of many local telephone companys regarding this dedicated central office service.

ANALOG VERSUS DIGITAL

At this point, it will be helpful to clarify some of the differences between analog and digital communications. Human speech is analog communication and is continuously variable in nature (Figure 4.14). Human speech can be viewed on an oscilloscope, an electronic device which visually displays electrical signals. Human speech resembles a complex alternating current wave form. The louder a person speaks, the greater the amplitude (height) of the wave. The shape of the wave varies in response to the various frequencies.

This complex analog wave form—human speech—is what the telephone system was designed to carry. Transmission is much more complex than the telegraph signal which preceded voice communications. Going from telegraph communications to voice communications was something like going from direct current to alternating current.

Human speech requires a much better transmission path than that required for telegraph communications, and is more difficult to transmit over long distances than telegraph signals. So, human speech presented a challenge to the early developers of local and long distance telephone systems.

With the advent of computers, zeroes and ones (off and on) as electrical pulses came into use. There is a vast difference between such pulses and the analog signal generated by human speech. Digital pulses are a reminder of the on and off signalling of telegraph systems.

The telephone network was not designed to carry digital computer pulses, and special equipment is needed to utilize the voice telephone network for communications. However, the telephone industry was aware of the increasing need for computer communications and that digital pulses have advantages over analog signals in terms of ease of transmission. The industry knew that it is possible to sample human

Analog Waveform

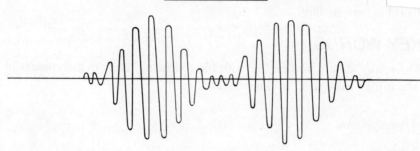

Figure 4.14. Human speech produces a complex analog wave form which varies constantly with the words being spoken. _____

speech at a rapid rate and still understand what is being said. So, switching matrices were developed based on passing these samples of the analog signal. These techniques for switching were similar to the sampling techniques used in time division multiplexing.

The next step in this evolution was to convert the analog samples into a series of true digital pulses which were similar to computer pulses. All of these digital pulses could be switched through the same digital switching matrix. The use of such matrices is the direction that has been selected for future growth of both central office and private switching systems.

The conversion of human speech into digital pulses first took place on long distance telephone transmission systems. A more recent step has been the introduction of all digital switches into central offices and PBX systems. However, the conversion process is slow. A great deal of money has been invested in the existing analog switches and no organization can afford to ignore the conversion expense.

The last area of conversion toward all-digital communications involves the wire from the telephone set to the central office. Changes have to be made in it to accommodate digital communications. This again is a slow and expensive process that cannot be done all at once.

The move toward an all-digital telecommunications network is often referred to as ISDN (Integrated Services Digital Network). Ideally, under this concept a digital PBX will have access to a digital central office over digital transmission facilities. Analog voice signals will be digitized at their source and all transmissions will be of digital information. Computer communications will remain in their original digital form and will greatly simplify computer communications.

Only time will tell how soon all of this will evolve and in what final form it will be offered to customers. However, the trend toward a digital world is here to stay.

KEY WORDS

The reader should be familiar with the following terms in the context in which they were used in this chapter:

Amplification

Analog

Area Code

Batteries

Busy Tone

Cable

Central Office

Centrex

Circuit

Common Control

Computer-Controlled

Connector Switch

Cord

Cross-Connect

Crossbar

Dial

Dial Tone

Diaphragm

Digit

Digital

Direct Current

Distribution Frame

Earphone

Electro-mechanical

Exchange Code

Frequency

Frequency Division Multiplexing

ISDN

Jack

Jumper

Key Telephone System

Line Finder Switch

Manual Switchboard

Microphone

Multiplexing

Numbering Plan

Off-Hook

On-Hook

Oscilloscope

PBX

Power

Progressive

Pulse

Ringing Current

Ringing Tone

Sampling

Selector Switch

Signalling

Step-by-Step

Switch Hook

Switching

Switching Equipment

Switching Matrix

Tandem Switch

Telephone

Test Equipment

Time Division Multiplexing

Tones

Traffic Engineer

Transmission

Transmission Equipment

Vibration

Wave Form

Wire

World Code

EXERCISES

1. How is human speech passed over telephone wires?

2. Why were dials placed on telephone sets?

3. Draw a diagram of the major sections of a telephone central office and explain the function of each section.

4. Why doesn't just one large central office building service an entire major metropolitan area?

5. How many pairs of wires are needed to connect eight subscribers to each other if a central switch is not used?

6. Why are new exchange codes formed?

7. What function does a connector switch perform in a step-by-step system?

8. How are common control switching systems more efficient than progressive switching systems?

9. What is the most basic telephone transmission medium?

10. Explain the difference between time and frequency division multiplexing.

11. Why is a key telephone system with hundreds of telephones not practical?

12. What similarities are there in the development of central office systems and PBX systems?

13. Why is there a move toward all-digital communications systems?

14. Will voice telephone calls ever be replaced entirely by computer communications?

5

Communication
with Computers

In Chapter 3, some of the applications for computers using telecommunications were discussed. This chapter will consider the technical aspects of computer communications.

The subject is somewhat complex because digital computer data has to utilize existing voice telephone channels, which are designed for analog communications. The adaptional process has required some technical ingenuity.

OVERVIEW

To adapt a large computer system to a telecommunications environment takes significant additional hardware and computer programs. This section provides an overview of the adaptional process, and following sections will provide more details regarding specific components of the system.

One of the main hardware devices added to a large computer system for telecommunications is a communications controller or front-end processor (Figure 5.1), an interface between the computer and the telecommunications channels. In a large computer system, the processor sits in a large cabinet on the computer room floor. The front-end processor is similar to a secretary who serves as an interface to a busy executive. The secretary receives incoming mail, opens it and places it on the executive's desk. After the executive has worked on the material, the secretary retrieves it, places it in an envelope and mails it.

The communications controller receives incoming data communications from a remote terminal and performs certain work on the incoming traffic before sending it on to the computer for processing. After the computer has done the actual data processing, the work is sent back to the controller where it is prepared for transmission back to the remote terminal.

The controller or front-end processor is a buffer device between the high-speed computer and the relatively slow telecommunications channel. The controller can analyze incoming data traffic for errors, perform code conversions, speed conversions, etc. Data communications from the computer can be arranged in the proper format for transmission to the distant terminal.

The communications controller can consist primarily of hardware components, but most controllers also contain software (computer programs). The term "front-end processor" is often used to describe controllers which contain software.

Within the central processing unit (CPU) is other software designed to interface with the communications controller and the telecommunications environment. All of this software gives the system tremendous capability. However, it also means that such systems can be quite complex to develop, install and maintain.

Application programs are installed in the CPU for specific data communications applications (remote order entry, airline reservations, etc). The communications controller and the telecommunications software are designed to isolate the application programs from the telecommunications environment. This helps to simplify the work of the application programmers in dealing with computer applications which involve data communications.

The communications controller interfaces the telecommunications

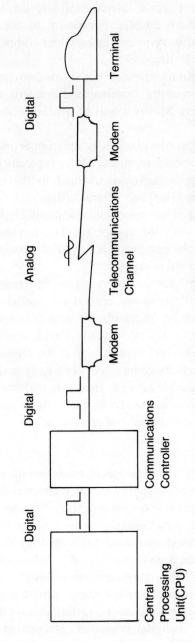

DATA COMMUNICATIONS SYSTEM

Central Processing Unit(CPU)

Digital

Communications Controller

Digital

Modem

Analog

Telecommunications Channel

Digital

Modem

Digital

Terminal

Figure 5.1. The major components of a data communications system. Digital data is converted into analog form for transmission over the telecommunications channel.

channel through a hardware device called a modem, which is a conversion device. It converts digital computer pulses into analog information that can be sent over voice telephone lines, the telecommunications channel. Modems have enabled computers to utilize the vast voice telephone network already in existence when computers needed a telecommunications capability.

A telecommunications channel has a modem at both ends of the channel. The modem at the terminal end converts analog information back into digital form. Modems will be discussed in greater detail later in this chapter.

The telecommunications channel is the connecting link between the computer and the remote terminals. It is typically a voice telephone channel, and can be a dedicated channel to the terminal or can be dialed-up through the telephone central office.

At the distant end of the telecommunications channel is the terminal that communicates with the computer. The terminal is the interface between people and the computer. It can be a teleprinter, video display, printer and/or a personal computer.

The physical path from the computer to the terminal is similar to a highway. Rules of the road are needed for traffic—data communications—to flow smoothly. Standards and protocols set the speed limit on the highway, assign rights of way, deal with mistakes, etc. Without them there could be no real data flow over the highway.

No telecommunications channel is ever totally perfect. Imperfections in the channel and problems with terminals and software can result in errors in data communications. To deal with these problems, many large computer systems have special test equipment.

MODEMS

The term "modem" is a contraction of modulator-demodulator. Modulation is the process of changing some characteristic of an electrical signal—called a carrier—in response to some other signal. A modem takes digital pulses from a computer or terminal and modulates a carrier which is sent to the modem at the other end of the channel (Figure 5.2). The modulated carrier is an analog signal which can be transmitted over the analog telephone telecommunications channel.

The carrier is a type of wave form which resembles alternating current and human speech. There are different ways that a carrier can be altered in response to digital computer information. This can include changing the amplitude, frequency, or phase of the carrier.

Changing the frequency is a form of modulation that is easy to under-

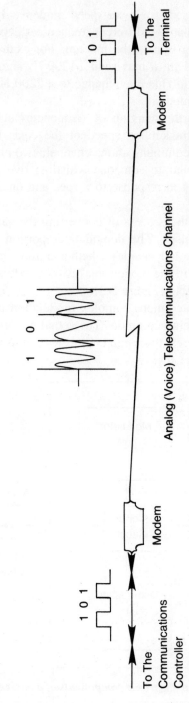

Figure 5.2. A modem (modulator/demodulator) converts computer data (zeroes and ones) into analog form for transmission over a voice telecommunications channel. A modem can also convert analog information back into digital form. This illustration shows modems using frequency modulation.

stand and widely used in slower-speed modems. In this technique the carrier is modulated at two different frequencies depending on whether a zero or one is being sent to the modem. For example, when a zero is received by the modem, it may send a 1200 Hz signal over the telecommunications channel. This may change to a 2200 Hz signal when a one is presented to the modem.

This back-and-forth changing of frequencies occurs at a rapid rate depending on the transmitted speed of the data. If someone were to listen in on the telecommunications channel, two changing tones would be heard. It is similar to someone whistling over the channel at two different frequencies in response to zeroes and ones from the computer or terminal.

Demodulation is the process of converting the varying analog signals back into digital pulses. The demodulator portion of the modem analyzes the variations and decides whether a zero or one is being sent. Electronic circuitry in the modem makes the modulation and demodulation capability possible (Figure 5.3).

At higher data rates more complex modulation techniques are used, phase modulation being common. The actual modulation techniques are usually of more interest to design engineers than users. The end-users of

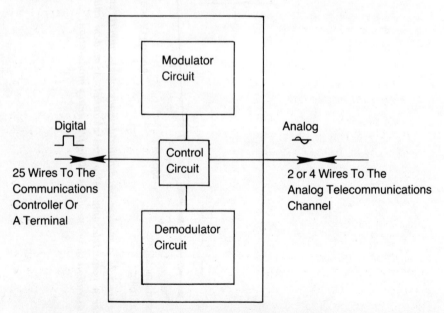

Figure 5.3. The main electronic components of a modem.

modems are primarily concerned with other characteristics of modems, such as speed. This is the rate at which the modem can send data over the telecommunications channel. Speeds range from approximately 300 bits per second (BPS) to 9,600 BPS and higher. A bit is the basic unit of measure in data communications; it stands for "binary digit." It is a zero or one which is all the computer understands. The number of BPS is used as a measure of transmission speed.

As one might expect, speed costs money. The higher the BPS, the more expensive the modem because it requires more complicated electronic circuitry. Slower data rates are often used when a low-speed terminal device is accessed directly by a human operator. For example, a teleprinter where an operator directly types in information to a remote computer might use a 300 or 1,200 BPS. Higher-speed modems might be needed when multiple terminals are using the same telecommunications channel or a high-speed printer is involved in receiving data from the computer. Then, 4,800 and 9,600 BPS modems are commonly found.

Modems are also classified in terms of the type of telecommunications channels on which they will be used. Low-speed modems—300, 1,200, and 2,400 BPS— are typically used with dial-up telecommunications channels through the telephone central office. Higher-speed modems—4,800, 9,600 BPS and faster— are typically used on dedicated telecommunications channels where a continuous channel links the computer and terminal.

The side of the modem which is connected to the computer or terminal has a 25-pin output connector. The side connected to the telecommunications channel has two or four wires (Figure 5.4).

Modems used in the dial-up telephone network have two wires, the same as a standard telephone set. Modems used on dedicated channels usually have four wires (two pairs). One pair of wires is used for sending data and the other pair for receiving it.

Modems come in all sizes and shapes. They can be mounted in a large box that sits on a desk or can be on a small printed circuit board mounted directly inside a terminal. Regardless of their size or shape, they perform the same basic functions.

Modems have to be compatible with each other. At lower speeds, modems from different vendors are often compatible. At higher speeds, compatibility is often more of a problem since different vendors often use different modulation techniques.

The death of the modem has been predicted for years, yet they are

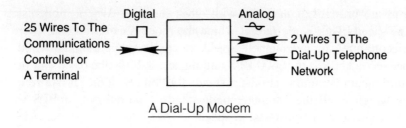

A Dial-Up Modem

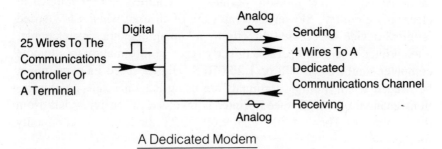

A Dedicated Modem

Figure 5.4. A modem which connects to the dial-up telephone network uses two wires (upper illustration). A modem which connects to a dedicated analog telecommunications channel usually has four wires (lower illustration). _____

still a fast-selling item. The move toward all-digital telecommunications is taking place at a slower rate than was anticipated by many people and so modems continue to be needed for the existing analog channels.

The price of modems has continued to decrease over the years. Along with decreasing prices has come a move on the part of users toward higher-speed modems. Once 300 BPS was considered adequate for dial-up use, and now users are moving up to 1,200 and 2,400 BPS modems. The higher speeds mean that less time is spent on dial-up calls. Particularly on long distance calls, the faster modems can pay for themselves in terms of reduced charges.

Modems are very reliable. The failures with them tend to occur in the first few hours of operation, and from then on the failure rate is low. The modem has made data communications possible, and they will be around for quite some time to come.

TELECOMMUNICATIONS CHANNELS

The telecommunications channel is the link among modems and ultimately the link between the computer and terminals. The channel is normally designed for human speech (analog communications). When the need for the remote accessing of computers via telecommunications first arose, a gigantic telephone network was already in existence. The modem was developed to adapt this existing network to computer communications.

One of the most widely used channels is a pair of wires to the local telephone company central office switch (Figure 5.5). A telephone number is assigned to the modem just as a telephone number is assigned to a telephone set. Both the terminal and computer could be connected to the same central office switch.

For the terminal user to access the computer, he simply dials up the telephone number for the computer. A dial-up connection is easily established on an as-needed basis.

A dial-up channel is typically a half duplex channel. This means that data can be sent in only one direction at a time. If both ends try to send data at the same time, there is a collision on the channel.

Some modems use a frequency division multiplexing technique (discussed in Chapter 4) to obtain a full duplex capability over a dial-up channel. With full duplex operation, the modems can send and receive at the same time. This is another method to obtain maximum utility of what is readily available.

When modems are connected over a dial-up channel, they go through a routine called handshaking. This is where the modems communicate with each other. The procedure has to occur on every dial-up call.

If problems arise on a dial-up call, it can be disconnected and re-dialed. This is what people do when they get a bad telephone connection. It is also a quick and easy procedure to use when problems occur on dial-up data communications.

Normally, when a full-time telecommunications channel is needed from the terminal to the computer, it is obtained in the form of a dedi-cated channel. Such a channel consists of a telephone circuit which does not pass through the central office switch, even though the wires do go through the central office (Figure 5.6). Rather, the wires are cross-connected on the distribution frame. Thus, the terminal and computer are always connected to each other.

Dedicated channels are often used when higher data speeds are needed, for higher volumes of traffic, or when the application requires a dedicated channel. For example, a terminal at a travel agency might be on a dedicated channel to provide instant access to information.

A dedicated channel saves the time of dialing each call, waiting for a connection to be established, for handshaking to occur, etc. This can be important in some computer applications.

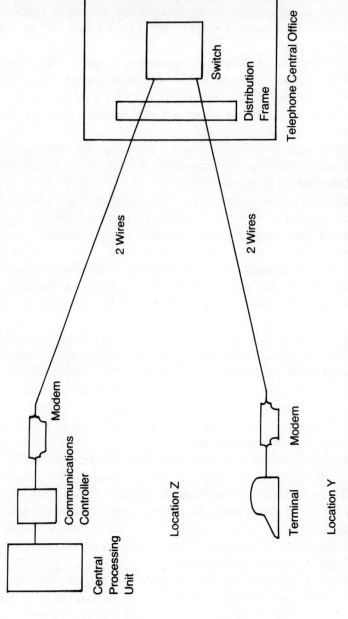

DIAL-UP TELECOMMUNICATIONS CHANNEL

Figure 5.5. A dial-up telecommunications channel is established through switching equipment in the central office.

DEDICATED TELECOMMUNICATIONS CHANNEL

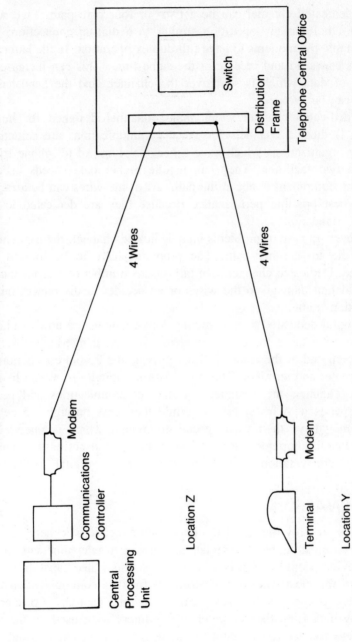

Figure 5.6. A dedicated telecommunications channel is established through only the distribution frame in the central office. The switching equipment is not used.

The dedicated channel can be a two- or four-wire path. Two wires provide a half duplex operation similar to a dial-up connection; four wires enable the modems to have full duplex operation. In the latter, the modems can send and receive at the same time. This can increase the volume of data which is sent over the channel, and the handshaking routine can be avoided.

The dedicated channel is an analog channel designed for human speech. Dedicated channels for voice communications are sometimes used by organizations which have a heavy volume of telephone traffic between two facilities. They can handle higher data speeds because switching equipment is not in the path. Also, the wires can be arranged for the best possible performance because they are dedicated to one specific connection.

However, in case of problems on a dedicated channel, the user cannot simply dial-up another path. The problems have to be located and corrected. Dedicated channels can fail for any number of reasons including accidental damage to the wires or an accidental disconnect on the distribution frame.

All-digital dedicated telecommunications channels are now available. They do not require the use of modems, but small interfacing devices are on each end of the channel. They provide the 25-pin connections to the computer and terminal. The signal is sent digitally from end to end.

These channels are designed for data communications and permit higher speeds with fewer errors. While they pass through the central office, they have their own special equipment which is intended to handle digital computer pulses. These channels will not pass an analog telephone conversation and are intended only for digital communications.

TERMINALS

Terminals are only the tip of the data communications iceberg, but are familiar to most people. Terminals are similar to telephone sets in that they provide people with access to a very sophisticated capability.

One of the most widely-used terminals for data communications is a teleprinter. It consists of a keyboard for sending data and a printer for receiving data from the computer. Teleprinters were used on the telegraph network as a replacement for the telegraph key. The original ones were rather large and contained electro-mechanical components. Gradually, teleprinters have become smaller and mainly electronic.

Teleprinters are often called "dumb" terminals because they do no local processing of the data. They simply send and receive. However, some of them have been made smarter by the inclusion of a very small computer. That permits the terminal to perform some local editing on data before it is sent to the computer.

A more sophisticated terminal is a cathode ray tube and a keyboard. These are called CRTs or video terminals. They permit the user to display information directly on a screen in response to commands entered on the keyboard, and are widely used when data needs to be observed but a printed copy is not needed. An airline reservation operator can use a video terminal to enter a request for flight information and to assign seats. Such terminals are normally used on dedicated telecommunications channels, often at the speeds of 4,800 or 9,600 BPS. The higher speeds are needed to quickly fill the screen with information.

A video display can have its own modem and dedicated channel. However, when multiple displays are in the same facility, a local communications controller is often installed (Figure 5.7). Multiple video terminals are connected to the controller, which is connected to the modem.

The local controller serves as a traffic manager for the terminals attached to it. It permits the video terminals to have their turn at sending and receiving from the remote computer. The controller is able to allocate time so that the users all think they have instant access to the computer. Cluster video controllers often have small computers built into them that enable them to perform more sophisticated functions.

When video terminals are used, there may be a need for printed copy. This can be provided by a printer. It is a terminal which receives data from the computer and prints it on paper.

A cluster controller might have one or more common printers to serve all of the video terminals. Printers often place heavy traffic demands on the system. The controller has to ensure that the printer does not overload the channel and thus prevent the video terminals from getting access.

A printer can also have its own dedicated channel. This might be the case when vast amounts of data are to be sent to the printer on a constant basis.

Computers can also be used as terminals. A medium-sized computer in a field location might do local data processing and then send the data to a large central computer for further processing. The connection between the two computers can be via a dial-up or a dedicated channel, depending on the volume of data to be sent and received.

Personal computers have also become terminals for data communications with large remote computers. The personal computer typically uses

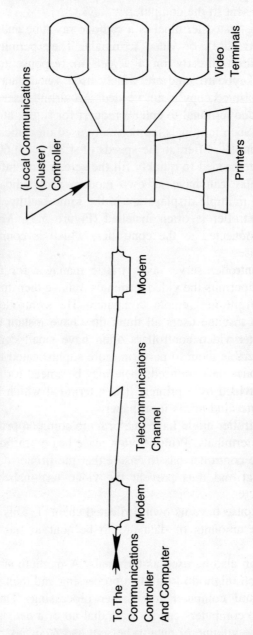

Figure 5.7. A local communications (cluster) controller permits multiple video terminals and printers to access one telecommunications channel.

a dial-up channel to call the remote computer. A modem can be built into the personal computer or it can be in a separate unit. Special programs are used to handle data communications with the remote computer.

One terminal that is often overlooked is a telephone set with a pad on it. In some applications, users can dial-up a computer and send data by pressing the buttons on the telephone pad. This application does not require modems since the pad generates tone signals which are analog in nature and pass directly over the channel.

STANDARDS AND PROTOCOLS

Standards and protocols make possible the transmission of computer communications over the telecommunications channel. These are the rules of the road. There are various aspects to these rules, but only a few will be considered in this section.

Data communications have to be coded for transmission. Sometimes the same code used in the computer is used for communications. In other cases, the internal computer code is converted to another code for data communications. EBCDIC (Extended Binary Coded Decimal Interchange Code) and ASCII (American Standard Code for Information Interchange) are among the codes used in data communications. As discussed in Chapter 3, codes are the zeroes and ones which represent numbers and letters.

In addition, codes are used to create control characters which are not normally considered by the user. For example, one control character may tell a printer that when it reaches the end of a line to go to the next line and start printing again at the far left side of the paper. Control characters are inserted without the user having to be concerned about them.

Codes are described in terms of the number of bits that it takes to make up a character. Computer codes typically consist of seven or eight bits. Within a computer, a character is typically handled in parallel fashion. This means that all the bits which make up a character are transferred at the same time.

Transmission over a telecommunications channel is in serial fashion, one bit at a time. The front-end processor at the central computer site converts data from parallel to serial form for transmission over the channel.

Encoded data can be sent asynchronously or synchronously over the channel. In asynchronous transmissions, every character stands on its own. A start-and-stop bit surrounds each character. This enables the

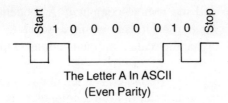

The Letter A In ASCII
(Even Parity)

Figure 5.8. In asynchronous transmission, start and stop bits surround each character, enabling each to stand on its own. _____

terminal and computer to remain in synch by analyzing one character at a time (Figure 5.8).

Asynchronous transmissions are usually used in low-speed applications, typically over a dial-up telecommunications channel. It is well-suited for applications where a human operator would type in letters and numbers at varying rates of speed. Each character can be considered on its own.

Asynchronous transmissions have a significant overhead since the start-and-stop information goes with every character. At higher speeds this overhead can become a burden and synchronous communications are typically used.

In synchronous communications, data is sent in blocks. Each block is preceded by information which indicates the start of a block. The end of each block contains information which indicates that it is the end of a block of data (Figure 5.9). Synchronous communications enable data to be sent with less overhead, but involve a more complex process and are normally used at higher speeds with sophisticated applications and over dedicated channels.

A number of speeds have become industry standards. They are 300, 1,200, 2,400, 4,800 and 9,600 BPS. Higher speeds of 14.4 kilobits per second (KBPS), 19.2 KBPS, 56 KBPS and higher are becoming more common. All-digital telecommunications channels will make higher data transmission rates more common.

The 25-pin connector which connects the modem to the computer or terminal is normally an RS232 interface. This is a standard interface developed by the Electronic Industries Association (EIA). It has helped to simplify the connection of terminals and computers to modems. The RS232 standard concerns itself primarily with the electrical connections on each pin, their purpose, etc. The handshaking routine between modems is related to the requirements of the RS232 standard to establish a connection between a computer and terminal.

Protocols are rules of how the data communications traffic will flow

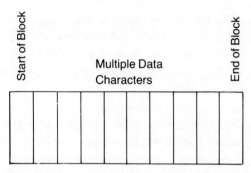

Figure 5.9. In synchronous transmissions, multiple data characters are sent within a block. Each block is surrounded by start-of-block and end-of-block information.

over the telecommunications channel. They are agreements on how data will be sent back and forth. One widely-used protocol for synchronous data communications is BSC (Binary Synchronous Communications). It was developed by IBM and has become a de facto industry standard. With BSC, data is sent in one direction at a time and one block at a time. BSC establishes rules regarding how this block transfer will take place. Even though the transfer is half duplex, a four-wire dedicated channel is typically used. This is done because after each block is received the sending location must be advised of this fact. Having a full duplex channel speeds up this acknowledgement and the transfer of data.

Newer protocols called HDLC (High-level Data Link Control) have come into existence. These protocols permit multiple blocks of data to be sent before an acknowledgement is required. Also, full duplex communications can take place over the channel providing a four-wire communications channel is available.

The newer protocols are also better suited for transmissions over satellite channels; however, the older protocols will remain in existence for many years. Organizations are often in no rush to convert because of the expense involved in replacing equipment and software.

ERROR DETECTION TECHNIQUES

There are a number of reasons for problems in data communications. For example, noise on the telecommunications channel can affect communications. When two people talk to each other, they can often ignore noise on the line, but this same noise can destroy the bits which make up data communications.

The faster the speed of data, the more damage that can be done by even an instant of noise on the channel. However, not only noise can affect data communications. Cross-talk—where a conversation on one telephone channel is picked up on another channel—can also have a negative impact on data communications. Also, attenuation—the loss of signal power—can cause errors.

When problems exist on a dial-up data call, the call can be disconnected and redialed. This is done at the start of a transmission when it is obvious that there are problems. However, problems often occur on a dial-up call after an initially good connection has been established. A brief instant of noise might affect only a few bits of data, but it is important for the user to know when this has happened.

There are a number of ways to deal with data communications errors. One technique, called parity checking, is a widely-used error detection technique, particularly in asynchronous communications. Parity relates to the evenness or oddness of the number of ones in the data code for any particular character. An illustration will help to clarify this technique.

The letter A in the ASCII code consists of the following seven bits: 1000001. If an even parity code scheme is used, the number of ones must come out even. In this case the number of ones is already even, so a final zero is added to give 10000010.

The letter C in ASCII is 1100001. The number of ones is odd. To make the parity even, a final one must be added to give a transmitted character of 11000011.

If a single error occurs in one of the transmitted data bits (a switch of 1 to 0 or vice versa) the parity bit check will catch the error. It cannot state which bit is in error, only that there is an error.

However, if two bits are switched, the parity bit will be fooled, so it is not a totally perfect technique. However, the switching of multiple bits might also result in a character that does not exist in the ASCII code and would thus be detected as an error.

Parity is a simple yet rather effective error detection technique. However, it adds an additional overhead bit for each seven bits of data that is transmitted. This increases the time for transmission and reduces the total volume of data that can be sent in a given period of time.

When data is transmitted in blocks, which is typically the case with synchronous communications, other error detection and correction techniques are used. One of these calls for the receiving location to send an acknowledgement after each block is received. The receiving location, after checking for errors, acknowledges that the block of data is all right and requests the next block of data. If errors are detected, the receiving location asks for a retransmission of the last block of data.

This block-checking technique helps to reduce the amount of overhead. It can be quite effective on telecommunications channels where line conditions are good and the likelihood of errors is low. However, on telecommunications channels where line conditions are poor and the error rate is high, there may be constant retransmissions of blocks of data.

The HDLC protocols allow multiple blocks to be sent before any acknowledgement is needed from the receiving location. The latter can advise in which specific blocks errors were detected and ask for retransmissions as required. This approach is often particularly effective when using satellite communications.

Through trial and error, users determine whether a particular telecommunications channel works effectively or not. When error rates become too high, other channels or protocols are adopted.

The move to all-digital telecommunications channels will help to reduce errors because the channels are designed for digital pulses. In an analog channel, an analog signal is amplified and reamplified throughout the transmission path. In a digital channel, new digital pulses can be generated rather than just amplifying the old ones. The final result is improved transmission performance.

TESTING

Unfortunately, even when errors are detected it is often difficult to know what is causing them. Often, the vendors of various services and equipment believe that the problem is somewhere besides in their equipment or service.

Many organizations which use data communications install their own testing equipment to help isolate and correct problems. This equipment can be manual or automatic in nature.

Many different types of equipment are involved in manual testing. Often, simple patch panels are installed on both the analog and digital sides of the modems at the computer location (Figure 5.10). A patch panel is a device which resembles a manual telephone switchboard. On the analog side, it has small holes for cords which resemble switchboard cords. On the digital side, 25-pin cables are needed. The patch panel permits spare equipment to be placed into service as needed.

Modems often have a built-in test capability. One such capability can generate a data transmission to see if the modem is working correctly. Another test involves sending a data test pattern to the modem at the distant end of the channel and having data sent back to the originating modem. Modem tests normally require that the data communications traffic be suspended while the tests are being conducted.

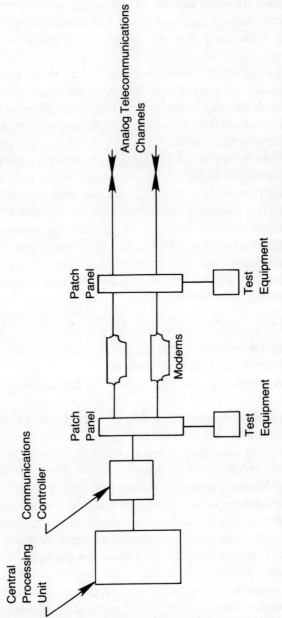

Figure 5.10. Patch panels permit test equipment to be connected as needed and also permit spare equipment to be placed into service.

A separate test unit called a bit error rate tester (BERT) can generate data communications which can be sent through an entire telecommunications channel—including the modems—to analyze the error rate. This is a more sophisticated test than that normally provided with a modem. The channel must be interrupted to conduct the tests.

Analog testing involves various types of equipment which are used to analyze the characteristics of the analog voice channel. This equipment is used to determine if the channel meets certain standards. If not, this can result in transmission errors.

Equipment is also available to analyze the normal data communications traffic flow. Often called protocol monitors, this equipment is placed between the modem and the computer communications controller and provides a visual display of the data traffic. It also displays information not normally seen, including control and protocol information. Data communications are not interrupted by this test.

Protocol monitors can help determine if the problems are in the data flowing over the channel rather than with the channel itself. For example, a distant terminal may generate transmissions that are faulty. Other versions of this test equipment can generate data transmissions to simulate various types of terminals, computers, protocols, etc.

Response time is often a concern in data communications. This is the amount of time it takes for the user to get a response from the computer after data is entered on a terminal. Response time test equipment permits the central computer site personnel to determine the response time over any channel and to more effectively analyze problems.

There is also automatic equipment which constantly monitors the channels for problems. This equipment is often part of newer modems. Each distant modem has special electronic circuitry which constantly advises a central control system at the computer site regarding the status of the channel. When problems are detected, the operator is automatically advised. Manual test equipment is then used to help isolate and correct the problem. This helps to better utilize the time and skills of trained operators and test personnel.

This automatic equipment monitors the channel, not the data traffic flowing over it. The monitoring activity occurs along with the normal data traffic and does not interrupt it.

As data communications systems utilize more and more terminals, users are finding it increasingly necessary to add sophisticated test equipment. In addition, skilled personnel are needed to operate this equipment, often on an around-the-clock basis. Problems, particularly those of an intermittent nature, can be very difficult to isolate. Many different personnel may be involved on complex problems, including central office test personnel, repair personnel at the terminal location, the modem vendor, etc. Just coordinating all the personnel can itself be a major problem.

So, written records are needed regarding when the various vendors were contacted and when they were dispatched to terminal locations. Large data communications systems require constant record-keeping. In addition, new installations and changes to existing equipment have to be coordinated, which means more paperwork. This paperwork and documentation is often computerized. A person at the computer site may enter a trouble report on a video terminal. The record can be called back to the screen as needed during the day. At the end of the day, written summary reports can be generated regarding problems, new installations, etc.

KEY WORDS

The reader should be familiar with the following terms in the context in which they were used in the chapter:

Analog

ASCII

Asynchronous

Attenuation

BERT

Bit

Block

BPS

BSC

Buffer

Carrier

Cluster Controller

Code

Communications Controller

Control Character

Cross-Connect

Cross-Talk

CRT

Date Communications

Dedicated Channel

Demodulation

Dial-Up

Digital

Distribution Frame

Dumb Terminal

EBCDIC

EIA

Errors

Frequency

Frequency Modulation

Front-End Processor

Full Duplex

Half Duplex

Handshaking

Hardware

HDLC

Interface

Modem

Modulation

Parity

Parallel

Patch Panel

Personal Computer

Phase Modulation

Printer

Protocol

Response Time

RS232

Series

Software

Standards

Start-and-Stop Bit

Synchronous

Telecommunications Channel

Telephone Set

Teleprinter

Terminal

Testing

Video Display

EXERCISES

1. What is the function of a communications controller?

2. Draw a diagram of a data communications path from a terminal to a computer and briefly explain the purpose of each major component in the path.

3. Why are modems necessary?

4. Explain modulation and demodulation.

5. Name the two main types of telecommunications channels.

6. Explain the difference between a two- and four-wire channel.

7. Why are there different types of terminals?

8. How can a telephone set be used as a terminal for data communications?

9. Explain the differences between asynchronous and synchronous communications.

10. What is the purpose of a data communications protocol?

11. Why can noise on a channel affect data communications?

12. Explain the use of parity as an error detection technique.

13. Explain the differences between manual and automatic test equipment.

14. Why can data communications problems be difficult to solve?

6

Radio

This chapter considers some of the fundamentals on which radio communications is based. Radio is often associated with radio broadcasting, but there are other aspects which need to be understood. Radio plays an important part in long distance telecommunications which will be considered in Chapter 8.

Television—discussed in Chapter 7—is built on radio waves and radio systems. So, radio is fundamental to many aspects of telecommunications.

The reader should find this chapter interesting reading since much of it can be easily related to technology which is seen in everyday life.

RADIO WAVES

Radio waves are all around us but cannot be detected by human senses, unlike heat or light waves which are easily detected.

119

Radio waves are electromagnetic radiations. They pass through space at the speed of light, are generated by a source called a transmitter, and are sent into space from an antenna. The transmitter sends alternating current into the antenna. This current alternates at much higher frequencies than the alternating current electricity found in a home. When this current passes back and forth through an antenna, electromagnetic energy spreads out from the antenna at the speed of light.

An electromagnetic field is thus created around the antenna. The changing nature of the field, as a result of the alternating current, produces electromagnetic waves—radio waves—which are radiated into space.

The commonly-used analogy for this radiation is to drop a stone into a still pond and see the waves radiate outward. The energy of the falling stone transfers itself into radiated waves in the water.

Radio waves are described in terms of their frequency. This is the same term that was used in Chapter 2 with alternating current electricity, and it means the same for radio waves. However, the frequency of the changes of radio waves often occur thousands and even millions of times per second, while alternating current electricity in a home has a frequency of 60 Hz (cycles per second).

There is a fundamental relationship between the frequency of a radio signal and its wavelength. The wavelength is the distance a radio wave travels from the transmitting antenna before another current surge in the antenna starts a second wave (Figure 6.1). It is inversely proportional to its frequency—the higher the frequency of the radio wave, the shorter its wavelength. This simply means that at higher frequencies, the waves come quite rapidly, one after the other. Therefore, the preceding wave cannot have traveled very far before the next wave is generated from the antenna. Wavelength can be calculated by a mathematical formula (Figure 6.2).

Terms commonly used when talking about the frequency of radio waves are kilohertz (KHz) and megahertz (MHz). One kilohertz is 1,000 Hz (cycles per second) and one megahertz is 1,000,000 Hz. At very high radio frequencies, the term gigahertz (GHz) is also used. One gigahertz is 1,000,000,000 Hz.

A radio wave in space can be intercepted by a receiving antenna. Since the wave is electrical energy it can set up an induced alternating current voltage in the receiving antenna. The voltage in the antenna is at the same frequency as that in the transmitting antenna. This induced voltage is very weak but can be detected by radio receiving equipment.

The early generating source for the alternating current fed into the

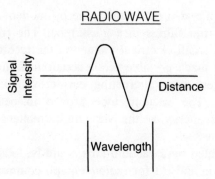

RADIO WAVE

Figure 6.1. The wave form for a radio signal resembles the wave form for alternating current electricity discussed in Chapter 2. _____

antenna was an electrical spark. An analogy of the early spark transmitters are the spark plugs and ignition system in an automobile. If this ignition system is not properly shielded, it can generate noise which will interfere with the radio and even other nearby radios. The spark plugs generate sparks which can radiate an electrical signal through space.

Spark signals are a rather impure form of alternating current energy. Yet, if connected to an antenna, they can transfer this energy into the antenna and cause a radio wave to be sent through space for reception at a distant location. By turning this spark signal on and off with a telegraph key, telecommunications can be sent through space. As primitive as it sounds today, this is how early radio signals were sent through space for many years.

Improved means of generating spark signals involved electromechanical alternators and arc generators, which could produce purer spark signals. However, spark was limited in its effectiveness and was not suited for radiotelephone communications.

On the receiving end, methods for detecting spark signals from the

WAVELENGTH

$$\lambda = \frac{300,000}{f}$$

λ is the wavelength in meters
f is the frequency in kilohertz (KHz)

Figure 6.2. The wavelength can be calculated by this formula when the frequency of the radio wave is known. (λ is the Greek letter lambda.) _____

receiving antenna were also rather primitive by modern standards. One technique involved iron filings in a glass tube. The filings moved in response to the very small electrical voltage in the receiving antenna.

The vacuum tube made possible the generation of continuous waves (CW). This is a very pure alternating current signal which is at a constant frequency. The vacuum tube proved to be well-suited to generating electrical energy at the very high frequencies needed for radio communications.

The energy generated by a vacuum tube could be fed directly into an antenna and keyed on and off for radiotelegraph communications. This type of signalling is often referred to as CW communications. *(In land based telegraph systems a telegraph key is used to send Morse code signals via wires. In radiotelegraph communications a telegraph key is used to send Morse code signals via radio waves).*

Vacuum tubes also are good detectors of radio waves, and can amplify radio signals. The conversion to vacuum tubes impacted both transmitting and receiving equipment.

Another advantage of the continuous waves generated by vacuum tubes is that they are suitable for the transmission of human speech (radiotelephony). The technique used to generate a radiotelephone signal is called modulation. (This term was discussed in Chapter 5 in reference to using modems for computer communications.)

To generate a voice transmission, the continuous wave signal—rather than being turned on and off—is simply left on. It now becomes a carrier for the human speech which is applied to it through the process of modulation.

Amplitude modulation was one of the original techniques used for voice transmissions. The amplitude of the radio signal is varied in response to human speech. In the U.S., the term AM radio means that amplitude modulation (AM) is being used.

Frequency modulation was later developed as another modulation technique. It provides better fidelity but requires more bandwidth. Again in the U.S., the term FM radio means that frequency modulation (FM) is being used.

FREQUENCY SPECTRUM

Understanding the radio frequency spectrum is very helpful in understanding radio communications. The radio frequency spectrum is a finite resource. The starting point is approximately 3 KHz and the ending point is approximately 300 GHz. This sounds like a significant amount of spectrum, yet parts of it have become congested.

The radio frequency spectrum can be divided into sections which have similar characteristics. This helps to simplify the understanding of the subject (Figure 6.3).

Starting at the low end of the radio spectrum are the low and very low frequencies (LF and VLF), approximately 3 KHz to 300 KHz. These frequencies were originally used for long distance spark communications. Today, this part of the radio frequency spectrum is used for radio navigation signals and for certain military communications, particularly with submerged submarines. At these frequencies the antennas are very large. They often have miles of wire, as those used for military communications. High power is needed for transmission over any significant distance. So, the use of these frequencies today for civilian applications is rather limited.

The medium frequencies (MF), approximately 300 KHz to 3,000 KHz, are used for maritime telecommunications. In the U.S., the MF range also contains the standard AM radio broadcasting frequencies, 535 KHz to 1,605 KHz.

AM radio stations have limited coverage, and typically serve specific cities. However, AM signals can often travel further at night over these frequencies. this will be discussed in Chapter 8.

The high frequency (HF) is approximately 3 MHz to 30 MHz. It is sometimes referred to as the shortwave range. These frequencies are used for international telecommucnications. They were originally considered to be worthless for long distance communications, but amateur radio operators discovered otherwise.

This frequency range is large yet very heavily occupied. It includes frequencies assigned for international shortwave broadcast stations. It is used for maritime and aeronautical telecommunications and contains many of the frequencies assigned to amateur radio operators.

The very high frequency (VHF) range, approximately 30 MHz to 300 MHz, contains many frequencies used for mobile communications. Radio waves at this frequency are normally limited to line-of-sight path. Police departments, fire departments, taxi cab companies, etc. have frequency assignments in this portion of the spectrum. In the U.S., VHF television is also in this range. These are channels 2 to 13 which are received on televisions sets. Each channel relates to a specific frequency assignment. The line-of-sight factor at these frequencies means that television stations in different cities can occupy the same channel and not interfere with each other.

Also in the VHF region are the FM radio stations. The wide bandwidth of FM radio and television signals can be more easily accommodated in this part of the radio frequency spectrum.

Next is the ultra-high frequency (UHF) part of the spectrum, approxi-

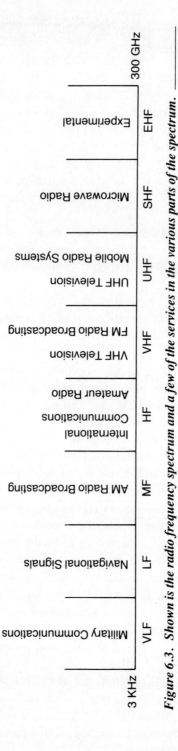

Figure 6.3. Shown is the radio frequency spectrum and a few of the services in the various parts of the spectrum.

mately .3 GHz to 3 GHz. It contains mobile radio frequencies. U.S. UHF television stations—channels 14 to 83—are also in this part of the spectrum. The UHF channels correspond to specific frequencies.

Finally are the super-high frequencies (SHF) and the extremely-high frequencies (EHS), approximately 3 GHz to 300 GHz. This range includes frequencies used for microwave radio communications and satellite communications (these will be discussed in Chapter 8).

Anyone willing to invest a few dollars in a multiple-band radio receiver will be able to pick up at least some of the frequencies in the various parts of the radio spectrum. Many people enjoy listening to international short-wave radio broadcasts, police communications, etc.

In some cases, transmitting stations are assigned a specific frequency. This is the case with radio and television broadcast stations. In other cases, several frequencies may be authorized for transmission. For example, a police department may have several different frequencies assigned to it.

A range of frequencies may be assigned to a certain type of operation. Amateur radio operators have a range of different frequencies; they can select specific frequencies within each assigned band of frequencies.

Interference is always a potential problem. Exclusive use of a frequency insures that there will be no interference. This is the case with radio and television broadcast stations. Amateur radio operators and others who share frequencies must cooperate with each other to avoid interference.

Call letters are assigned to transmitting stations for identification purposes. Radio and television broadcast stations are usually known by their call letters. Each amateur radio operator has his own set of call letters; W8QYR is an example of such call letters.

The International Telecommunications Union (ITU) in Switzerland coordinates frequency assignments world-wide. In the U.S., the Federal Communications Commission (FCC) regulates specific frequency assignments, the issuing of call letters, etc. in accordance with international agreements.

TRANSMITTING CIRCUITS

The basic transmitting circuit is the oscillator (Figure 6.4) that generates a continuous-wave radio signal. It can operate on a specific frequency and needs only a few electronic components. Being able to transmit on a specific frequency is an important consideration in radio communications.

There are two primary methods of determining the frequency of an

VARIABLE FREQUENCY OSCILLATOR

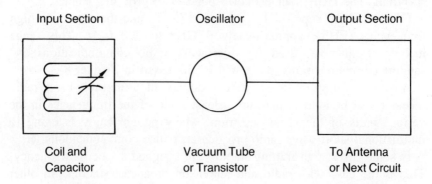

Input Section   Oscillator   Output Section

Coil and   Vacuum Tube   To Antenna
Capacitor   or Transistor   or Next Circuit

CRYSTAL-CONTROLLED OSCILLATOR

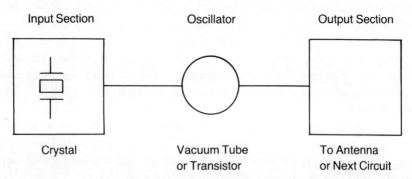

Input Section   Oscillator   Output Section

Crystal   Vacuum Tube   To Antenna
                            or Transistor   or Next Circuit

Figure 6.4. An oscillator circuit can generate a continuous wave radio signal. The frequency can be determined by a coil and capacitor or by a crystal. _____

oscillator circuit. One method involves using a coil and capacitor to form a tuned circuit which oscillates at one specific frequency. By using a variable capacitor the frequency can also be easily changed. This is advantageous when different frequencies are needed. The term variable frequency oscillator (VFO) is used to describe a tunable oscillator circuit.

An oscillator circuit oscillates because some of the output of the oscillator current is fed back to the input of the circuit to keep the oscillation going. An initial change, by the application of voltage, starts the oscillation process.

Frequency stability has always been one of the difficulties with oscillator circuits which use a coil and capacitor to determine the frequency of the oscillator. To achieve greater frequency stability, particularly when only one frequency is needed, a crystal is used on the input side of the oscillator circuit. This crystal is made of quartz and can vibrate to generate electrical voltage surges. The output energy fed back to the input of the oscillator shocks the crystal into vibrating. The crystal then generates electrical surges which keep the whole circuit oscillating at one specific frequency.

There are other techniques which use multiple crystals to obtain a large number of different frequencies. This provides the stability of crystals with the variability of frequencies which is often needed in many transmitters.

For some applications, the signals generated by an oscillator circuit can be used without further changes. An oscillator by itself can be used as a low-power radiotelegraph transmitter. A telegraph key can be used to turn the oscillator on and off to send radiotelegraph signals. Amateur radio operators have used oscillators, which generate only a few watts of power, to communicate over hundreds of miles.

However, for most radio transmitting applications, the signal from the oscillator circuit must be further amplified. This is done by using a radio frequency amplifier circuit. As the name implies, this circuit increases the power of continuous waves at radio frequencies to higher power levels.

Another type of circuit—a frequency doubler circuit—can increase the frequency of the oscillator circuit. The frequency can actually be doubled, tripled, etc. to reach very high frequencies. This approach has proven more effective than trying to generate the initial oscillations at higher frequencies.

Radio transmitters are described in terms of their power which is rated in watts. This is the same term used in Chapter 2 in regard to electricity, only now what is being considered is the electrical power which a transmitter can present to an antenna.

For purposes of comparison, amateur radio operators use transmitters which generate a few hundred watts. AM radio broadcast stations often use transmitters which generate thousands of watts. Television stations typically generate more transmitted power than AM radio stations. Like speed with modems, power in transmitters costs money.

To generate a voice transmission, the continuous wave carrier must be modulated. This is the case with amplitude modulation. Here, the human voice generates a weak variable electrical current by micro-

VOICE RADIO TRANSMITTER

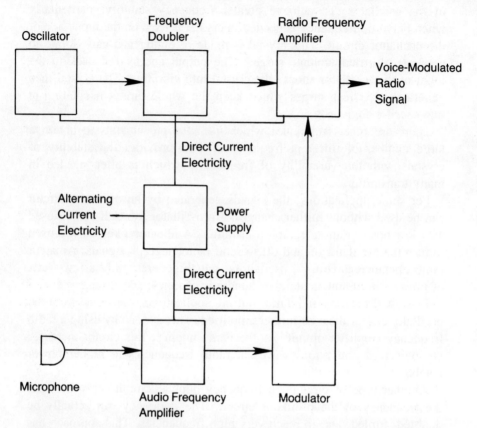

Figure 6.5. In a voice radio transmitter, an audio signal modulates the continuous wave carrier generated by the oscillator circuit. _____

phone. The current is amplified by audio amplifiers, similar to a public address system. The strong audio signal is then used to modulate the radio carrier (Figure 6.5); an analogy is the carrier being a train and the modulation a passenger. There are a number of different circuits which are used to achieve amplitude modulation, but the final result is that the amplitude of the carrier changes in response to human speech.

The process of amplitude modulation results in a radio signal which is wider than the original continuous wave carrier. This means that an AM signal takes up more space than a radiotelegraph signal.

Frequency modulation provides better fidelity for the transmitted audio signal but also produces a signal which is wider than an amplitude modulated signal. So, frequency modulation is more often used with VHF and UHF parts of the spectrum where space is less of a problem.

Even more sophisticated modulation techniques have been developed, one of them being single sideband (SSB). It is widely used on the high frequencies for international point-to-point telecommunications by aircraft, ships and amateur radio operators. SSB results in a voice signal which takes up less space than an amplitude modulated signal. However, SSB requires sophisticated modulating circuits and more sophisticated receiving equipment.

Power supplies in transmitting equipment convert alternating current into the direct current needed by transmitter circuits. The radio transmitter then generates alternating current but at radio frequencies.

RECEIVING CIRCUITS

The development of electronic circuits which can detect and receive radio waves progressed along with the development of transmitter circuits. One widely-used detector for early radio broadcasting was the crystal detector. This circuit uses a mineral called galena for the detector. It is well-suited for the detection of amplitude modulated radio signals and requires no external power source (Figure 6.6). Its operation is so basic that it is worth examining in detail.

Basically, the crystal detector is a demodulator. It takes the amplitude modulated signal and demodulates it to produce human speech in the earphones. If connected alone to an antenna and ground, the earphones produce no sound. This is because the frequency of the radio signal changes at such a rapid rate that the earphones are not able to follow these changes.

The crystal detector is a one-way device to radio waves. It permits changes to flow from the antenna to the ground. However, the return surge, caused by the alternating radio wave, can flow only one way through the earphones. The net result is that changes which follow the human voice at audio frequencies are slow enough to operate the earphones and produce sound.

To amplify weak radio radio signals before detection takes place, radio frequency (RF) amplifying circuits were developed. They are similar to the RF amplifying circuits found in transmitters. However, RF amplifiers in receivers involve only very low power levels, much lower than what are encountered in a transmitter. (Chapter 2 explains how vacuum tubes and transistors can amplify signals.)

The signal from a detector circuit, even with an RF amplifier, is suitable primarily to operate headphones. An audio frequency amplifier

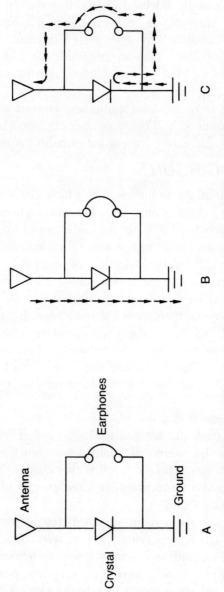

CRYSTAL RADIO RECEIVER

Figure 6.6. A crystal radio receiver can detect and demodulate amplitude modulated radio signals. Drawing A shows the basic circuit. Drawing B shows that the crystal permits changes in one direction to flow from the antenna to the ground. Drawing C shows that changes in the reverse direction are forced through the earphones.

circuit is used to amplify the signal from a detector. The audio signal can be amplified to a level strong enough to operate a loudspeaker.

Multiple RF and AF amplifier stages can be used to make a much more sensitive and selective receiver. Sensitivity and selectivity are two primary measures of receiver performance. Sensitivity is the ability of a receiver to pick up weak radio signals, and selectivity is its ability to separate one signal from another. By way of comparison, a basic crystal detector circuit is not very sensitive and lacks selectivity. It can be made somewhat selective by the addition of a coil and capacitor, but it cannot begin to compare with a multistage receiver.

To receive continuous-wave radiotelegraph signals, additional electronic circuitry is added to the multistage receiver. The final result is a receiver which is fairly effective for both domestic and international radio reception.

In the past, these receivers—with multiple stages of RF and AF amplification—often had many dials on the front panel. Each stage often had to be tuned for peak performance on a specific frequency. In the early days, in every home, someone was the "specialist" in operating the family radio.

An American, Edwin H. Armstrong, developed a new approach to radio reception, the superheterodyne receiver. This approach to radio reception is still used today. Standard AM and FM broadcast receivers are based on this principle (Figure 6.7).

In the superheterodyne receiver there is a very low-power oscillator circuit. It generates a radio frequency signal which is mixed with the incoming radio signal in a mixer circuit to produce a new radio frequency signal. This new signal is at an intermediate frequency (IF) which is constant for every received signal. It is lower than the original received radio frequency but is still not yet at audio frequencies.

The IF signal is passed through radio frequency amplifiers which operate only at the intermediate frequency: these are called IF amplifiers. Every incoming signal can be converted to a constant intermediate frequency because the frequency of the oscillator changes as the tuning knob is changed.

The IF signal is fed to a detector circuit which demodulates the signal to produce an audio signal. This signal can be amplified in audio amplifying circuits as needed.

The superheterodyne principle produces a receiver with greatly improved sensitivity and selectivity. It also makes one-dial tuning a practical reality and made radio receivers easy to operate by anyone.

To receive radiotelegraph signals (CW) on a superheterodyne re-

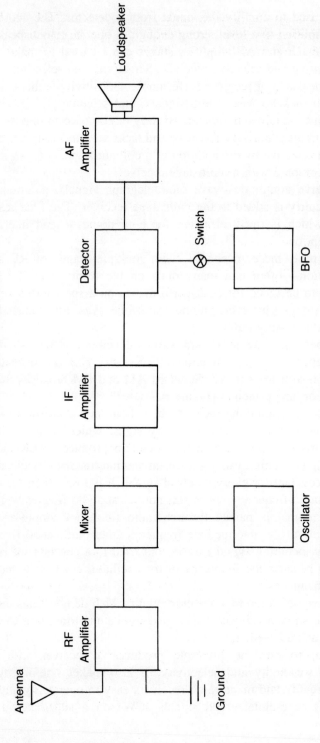

Figure 6.7. In a superheterodyne receiver, every incoming signal is mixed with a local oscillator signal to produce an intermediate frequency from which the audio signal is detected and amplified. The BFO is used only for radiotelegraph reception.

ceiver, another oscillator, called a beat frequency oscillator (BFO) is used. The BFO gives the radiotelegraph signal a tone which can be easily copied. Without the BFO, radiotelegraph signals appear as thumping noises.

MOBILE RADIO

Mobile radio systems are the transmitters and receivers used in automobiles, ships and aircraft. They are often called two-way systems since they are intended for point-to-point communications. This type of radio communication is widely used but not as well-known as AM and FM radio broadcasting.

A category of radio equipment called transceivers is often found in mobile radio systems. In a transceiver, both the transmitter and receiver are contained in one unit. Some electronic circuits are common to both the transmitter and receiver.

Frequently, mobile radio transmitters and receivers are mounted in the trunk of an automobile. Under the dashboard is a control unit which operates the equipment. This systems keeps the under-dashboard area free of the clutter of the transmitter and receiver.

Mobile radio systems often operate at very high and ultra-high frequencies. Some systems operate on only one frequency, while others have multiple channels which correspond to specific frequencies. The systems are normally used for voice communications to a base station. Their low power and the use of line-of-sight frequencies makes it difficult for mobile systems to communicate with each other.

Some mobile radio systems are now also being used for data communications. A data terminal is installed in the mobile unit. The communications are sent and received via radio waves. The terminal might consist of a teleprinter with a keyboard for entering a message to the mobile transmitter and a printer for displaying the message from the receiver.

To communicate with a mobile unit in an automobile, a high power base station is needed. It is the central point which can contact all of the vehicles. The base station at very high and ultra-high frequencies has a line-of-sight path to the mobile vehicles. Often, the transmitting and receiving antennas are on top of a building or tower. The base station operations personnel may be remotely located from the transmitter and receiver, and may be connected to the equipment via a dedicated telephone channel (Figure 6.8).

Some base stations are designed as repeaters. They are intended to permit mobile stations to access each other directly through the repeater.

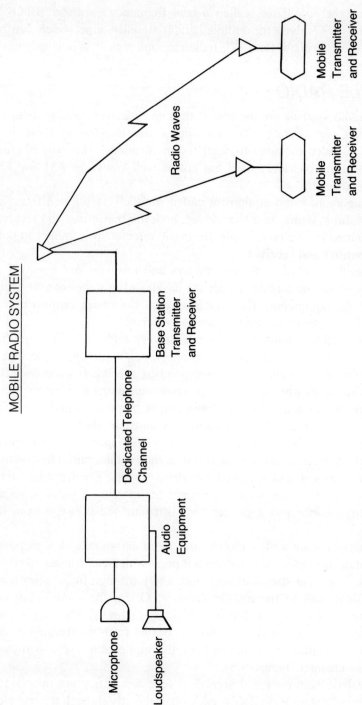

Figure 6.8. In a mobile radio system, a high-power base station is used to communicate with the mobile systems. The base station transmitter and receiver are often remotely located from the personnel operating the station.

In a repeater operation, all mobile stations listen on the same frequency but transmit on another frequency. The repeater receives the relatively low-power signal from a mobile station and rebroadcasts it on the repeater transmitting frequency. This enables all of the other mobile stations to easily pick up the signal (Figure 6.9).

Repeaters also permit very low-power hand-held transceivers to contact each other though they may be many miles apart. This greatly increases the flexibility of small-radio communications systems.

Mobile telephone systems in automobiles were once a luxury item that was difficult to obtain. The original systems used one central base station which could operate on only a few channels. So, in metropolitan areas, even those who had a telephone in an automobile often found getting a free channel to place a call a difficult process.

Now, thanks to cellular radio, mobile telephone service is becoming more widely available. With the cellular technique, a city is divided up into cells. Within each cell there is a low-power base station which uses

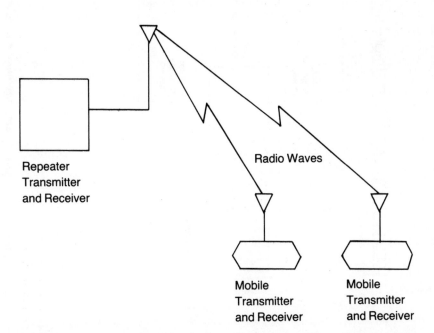

Figure 6.9. In a repeater radio system, low-power mobile systems can communicate with each other via the repeater station.

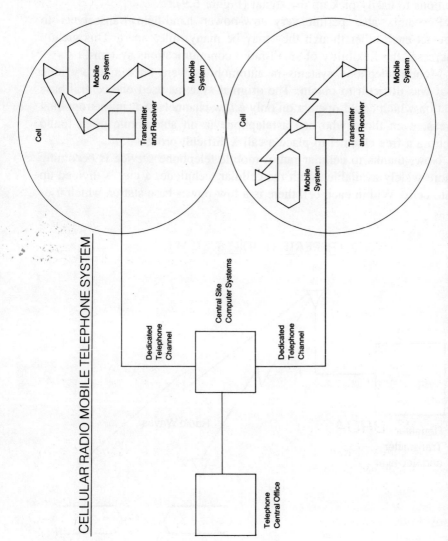

CELLULAR RADIO MOBILE TELEPHONE SYSTEM

Figure 6.10. In this system, any mobile telephone has access to telephone service through the cell transmitter and receiver.

a number of frequencies for communications with the vehicles within the cell. Other cells use the same frequencies, and this enables a rather limited number of frequencies to effectively serve a city and a large number of mobile telephone subscribers (Figure 6.10).

All of the cells are connected to a central site via a dedicated telephone channel. The central site provides access to the local telephone central office. A computer system at the central site coordinates the activity of the entire system. The computer—via the various cells—is able to advise computers in the mobile systems regarding what channels to use for transmitting and receiving.

The frequencies used by the mobile systems change under computer control as the vehicle moves from one cell to another. All of this happens automatically; the user does not have to make any frequency changes. The net result is a system that is as effective and easy to use as a home telephone.

Radio communications with boats and ships is also a widely-used form of mobile communications. Ships at sea still often use radiotelegraphy on high frequencies to contact a land base station. In some cases, radio teleprinters are replacing the telegraph keys.

For radiotelephone communications with ships, single sideband (SSB) is widely used. It provides a means of interactive voice communications.

Smaller ships and boats which operate closer to shore and on inland waterways often use very high frequencies for two-way voice communications with base stations and with each other. The line-of-sight communications at these frequencies are usually adequate for their needs. Aircraft also use very high frequencies for air-to-ground communications.

RADIO BROADCASTING

The one area of radio communications with which everyone is familiar is AM and FM radio broadcasting. It is part of almost every person's life in the U.S.

The starting point for radio broadcasting is the broadcast studio, which is often separate from the transmitting site (Figure 6.11). An announcer sits before a microphone in the studio. Broadcast microphones are high-quality devices intended to obtain the best speech quality. The studio itself is soundproofed to insure the best acoustical qualities.

The micorphone is connected to an audio console where the weak electrical energy generated by the microphone can be amplified and

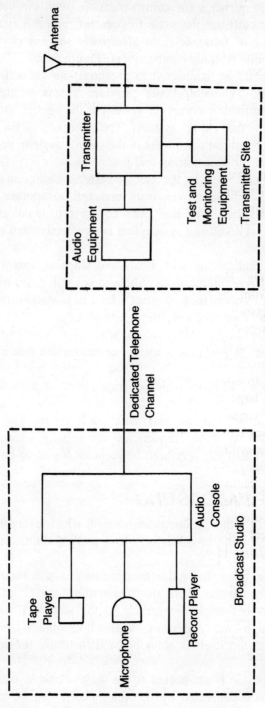

Figure 6.11. In this system, the studio and transmitter are often at different locations and are connected by a dedicated channel.

monitored. Also connected to the console are record and tape players that play prerecorded music, commercials, announcements and programs.

The audio console is also a switching center where the announcer or other studio personnel can select the record players, microphones, tape players, etc. that will be connected to the transmitter. If the station is affiliated with a network, the programming from the network enters the console over a dedicated telephone channel or satellite channel.

Remote broadcasts, which take place outside of the studio, are connected to the studio audio console. These broadcasts can come in over a telephone channel or via a mobile radio system.

The studio personnel control the console and the sequence of programming. In smaller stations the announcer operates the console; in larger stations a separate studio engineer might control it.

The signal from the console is sent to the transmitter for broadcast via radio waves. The studio and transmitting equipment can be located in the same building. However, in many cases the transmitter is located several miles from the studio. The remote location of the transmitter might be necessary to obtain sufficient space for the transmitting antenna. The signal from the studio is sent to the transmitter over a dedicated telephone channel.

At the transmitter site there is additional audio equipment to amplify the signal. The transmitter is contained in a large cabinet which sits on the floor. Very large transmitters may be contained in several cabinets. The transmitter contains the modulation equipment necessary for amplitude or frequency modulation.

Broadcast transmitters are crystal-controlled because they operate on only one frequency. Radio broadcast transmitters are designed to transmit high-quality radio signals. A transmitter site may have both AM and FM transmitters if the station is licensed for both types of operation.

The broadcasting of stereo music on FM radio has brought a new level of technical sophistication to radio signals. Stereo music requires left and right channels which are played in left and right speakers in a stereo music system.

To broadcast stereo signals, an FM station transmits these two separate channels over one radio carrier. This is accomplished by multiplexing, which permits more than one channel to be broadcast over one FM signal. (Multiplexing was discussed in Chapter 4.) The multiplexing used for FM stereo is a type of frequency division multiplexing.

In addition to broadcasting a second channel for stereo music, an FM radio station can broadcast another channel that can be used for special transmissions unrelated to normal programming. It can be used to broadcast continuous music, time signals, data communications, etc. To receive this channel, special receiving equipment is required. This equipment is not available to the general public. It is available only to individuals who are authorized to receive the information on the channel.

The transmitter site also contains test and monitoring equipment to insure that the transmitter power, frequency, amount of modulation, etc., are all within standards. In the past, transmitter sites were staffed with technical personnel. This was often a lonely job, particularly when the transmitter site was located far out in the country or on top of a mountain. Today, transmitter sites are often unattended. Their operation is monitored remotely from the broadcast studio. Monitoring information is sent back over a dedicated telephone channel to the studio. Repair personnel are dispatched to the transmitter site only when problems arise.

ANTENNAS

Antennas are a fascinating topic. At times they rank with alternating current electricity for something which can be difficult to understand. This is particularly the case with complex antenna systems used for certain types of AM radio broadcasting and international shortwave broadcasting. Yet, an antenna has the rather straightforward function of radiating radio frequency energy into space.

The size and type of antenna used for transmitting or receiving is closely related to the frequency being used. The lower the frequency, the longer the wavelength and the larger the antenna.

At the low and very low frequencies, antennas are often made of wire which is strung between towers. The towers are support structures to get the wire in the air. At these frequencies, antenna systems can consist of miles of wire.

At medium frequencies, wire strung between towers can also be used as an antenna. However, the amount of wire needed is considerably less than what is required at lower frequencies. The length of the wire can be considered in terms of hundreds of feet rather than thousands of feet or miles.

AM broadcasting stations which operate in this frequency range use vertical towers as an antenna. This approach helps to generate the type of signal that is conducive to AM reception.

In a basic AM antenna system, one vertical tower serves as the antenna. The tower is insulated from the ground. Transmitter power is fed directly to the base of the tower which can be several hundred feet high, depending on the frequency of operation of the AM station. Surrounding this tower and buried in the ground are a large number of copper wires called a ground screen that helps to improve the radiating efficiency of the antenna.

A one-tower vertical AM antenna radiates a signal uniformly in all directions. By using multiple vertical towers, it is possible to shape the pattern of the radiated signal. This technique is often used to weaken the signal in certain directions to prevent interference with other stations on the same frequency in other cities. This is accomplished by passing the radio frequency signal from the transmitter through coils and capacitors before the signal reaches the various vertical towers. The phase of the alternating current is affected by the coils and capacitors. This results in signals at the various towers which are out of phase with each other, and produces a radiated signal which is strong in some directions but weak in others (Figure 6.12).

At the high frequencies, the antenna is often wire-strung between towers. Such antennas are well-suited for radiating signals which will travel great distances at these frequencies. An antenna of approximately 150 feet can be very effective.

At the higher end of this part of the radio frequency spectrum, an antenna can take on an entirely new form. It can become a beam antenna which is a larger version of the antennas found on homes in the early days of television. A beam antenna is very directional. By rotating it, the transmitted signal can be sent in one specific direction. They are widely used for point-to-point commercial radio communications over great distances.

At the high frequency range, some international stations also use sophisticated wire antenna systems which are mounted between towers. These antennas can be made highly directional. Often, multiple antennas are used for transmissions to different parts of the world.

At the very high and ultra-high frequencies, antennas become much smaller. For mobile operations a small vertical wire is often mounted on the vehicle. Such antennas can be seen on police cars and taxicabs. The transmitting antennas at the base station for these frequencies may be just a vertical wire. However, because of the small size of antennas at these frequencies, more complex antennas are often used. They will often be mounted on a tower or high building to get the maximum coverage of a given area. The tower is not part of the antenna system and does not have to be insulated from the ground like an AM antenna.

Small boats and aircraft which operate at these frequencies have small

DIRECTIONAL ANTENNA SYSTEM

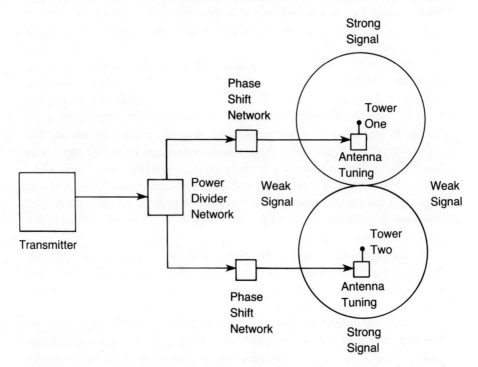

Figure 6.12. Here, the radio frequency signal from the transmitter is passed through networks of coils and capacitors before it is fed to two or more vertical towers. _____

antennas. Particularly in the case of aircraft, the antenna must not interfere with the aerodynamics of the craft.

Microwave radio systems, to be discussed in Chapter 8, have antennas which resemble large horns. These antennas greatly concentrate radio energy for transmission in one direction, and are seen when driving cross-country.

A transmission line is used to transfer the transmitter power to the antenna system. A transmission line can be a single electrical wire surrounded by insulating material and a metal sheath. This is called a coaxial cable.

Often the same antenna is used for transmitting and receiving. In some cases, different antennas are needed. Transmitting antenna must be able to effectively handle the amount of power being presented to them. Receiving antennas, however, deal with only very low levels of received energy.

KEY WORDS

The reader should be familiar with the following terms in the context in which they were used in this chapter:

Amateur Radio

Amplitude Modulation

Antenna

Audio

Audio Console

Audio Frequency Amplifier

Base Station

BFO

Broadcasting

Capacitor

Carrier

Cellular Radio

Channel

Coaxial Cable

Coil

Continuous Waves (CW)

Crystal

Detector

Directional

Earphone

Electromagnetic Radiation

EHF

FCC

Frequency

Frequency Doubler

Frequency Modulation

Frequency Spectrum

GHz

HF

Hz

Interference

Intermediate Frequency

ITU

KHz

LF

Loudspeaker

MF

MHz

Microphone

Mobile Radio

Modulation

Multiplexing

Multistage

Oscillator

Radio Frequency Amplifier

Radiotelegraph

Radiotelephone

Radio Waves

Receiver

Repeater

Selectivity

Sensitivity

SHF

Shortwave

Spark

SSB

Stability

Superheterodyne

Teleprinter

Transceiver

Transmission Line

Transmitter

Tower

UHF

VFO

VHF

VLF

Watt

Wavelength

Wire

W8QYR

EXERCISES

1. Why are radio waves invisible?

2. What are two advantages of vacuum tubes over spark communications?

3. Draw a diagram of the radio frequency spectrum and label the major frequencies.

4. Why are radio frequencies assigned?

5. Draw a diagram of a radio transmitter used for voice communications and explain the functions of the major components.

6. Explain the differences between a VFO and a crystal-controlled oscillator.

7. Draw a block diagram of a superheterodyne receiver and briefly explain the function of each circuit.

8. Name three advantages of a superheterodyne receiver.

9. Why are the antennas for mobile radio base stations often mounted on towers?

10. How is a broadcast studio connected to a remotely located transmitter?

11. How is stereo music transmitted over FM radio?

12. Why are different types of antennas often used at different radio frequencies?

13. How is a radio receiver connected to an external antenna?

7

Television

In the U.S., television is usually associated with TV broadcasting. However, television is also used for other purposes.

This chapter focuses on some of the technical aspects of television. The main focus is on a basic understanding of how pictures can be transmitted and received. This is a very complex process and only some of basic circuits and principles can be covered. While the emphasis is on basic black-and-white television, color transmissions are also explained. Color adds a new dimension to a television picture but involves increased technical complexity.

VIDEO SIGNALS

Chapters 4 and 6 explain how sound waves can be converted into electrical energy which can be sent over wires or via radio waves. Television takes the process one step further and enables full-motion pictures to be transmitted via electrical signals.

In an audio system, the sound waves operate a microphone to generate electrical energy which follows human speech. At the distant end the electrical energy is converted back to sound via a loudspeaker. To transmit television pictures, the lightwaves are detected by a television camera and converted to electrical energy which is converted to pictures on a picture tube.

The heart of a television camera is a cathode-ray tube (CRT), a vacuum tube. Light from the visual scene strikes the tube just as it does the human eye. Different objects give off different intensities of light; a dark object sends out less light energy to the camera tube than a bright object.

On the face of the camera tube falls a picture whose intensity varies depending on the amount of light sent from the different parts of the visual scene. The face of a camera tube is photoconductive and exhibits changes in electrical conductivity depending on the amount of light which strikes it. These changes have to be detected to transmit a simple black-and-white picture.

In the camera tube, the cathode generates an electron stream similar to that in a vacuum tube. The electron stream or beam has to scan the entire face of the tube. It is this movement of the beam that results in the detection of the visual scene on the face of the camera tube and results in an electrical representation of the visual scene. Different types of television camera tubes use variations of this technique to obtain the same final result.

The electron beam in a camera tube, like any other electron stream, can be affected by a magnetic field. So, this field is used to move the electron beam across the screen one line at a time to scan the entire screen (Figure 7.1). This process happens at a very rapid rate.

Variations in electrical voltages are generated in the scanning process. They correspond to the amount of light being reflected onto the screen of the camera tube. These variations form an analog signal whose intensity is constantly varying in response to the amount of light being detected. The variations seen on the camera tube can be relayed to a picture tube for a reproduction of the original scene. A picture tube is another glass cathode ray tube in which changes in electrical intensity —corresponding to the picture being viewed—must be used to produce the black-and-white television picture.

In a picture tube, an electron beam is generated from the cathode. The beam must move across the screen to reproduce the video signal being viewed by the camera tube. Again, a magnetic field causes the electron beam to move across the face of the screen from left to right.

HORIZONTAL SCANNING

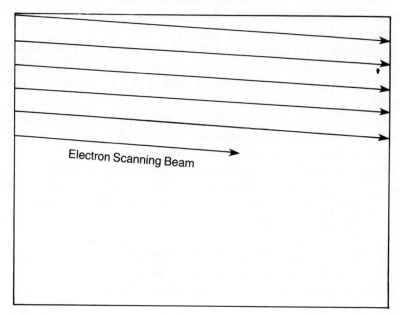

Figure 7.1. A magnetic field is used to move the electron scanning beam across the screen of a camera or picture tube, one line at a time. _____

(If the reader doubts that a black-and-white television picture is made up of lines, he can use a magnifying glass to look at the face of a black-and-white tube when the television set is on but not tuned to a station. The lines will be clearly visible.)

To reproduce the electrical variations which correspond to the light intensity of the original picture, the video signal from the camera tube causes the strength of the electron beam in the picture tube to vary. Variations in the beam are caused by the video signal received from the camera tube being applied to the grid of the picture tube. The grid controls the strength of the electron flow just as it does in any vacuum tube.

A television picture tube has a fluorescent screen which gives off light in response to the electron beam generated by the cathode. The strength of the light on the screen is determined by the strength of the beam which is determined by the signal applied to the grid of the picture tube.

So, a moving electron beam in the camera tube results in a moving beam in the picture tube that reproduces the picture viewed by the camera. The movement of the beam is the result of coils of wire around the neck of the picture tube. Electricity through these coils generates the magnetic field which moves the beam.

By this very basic process, a black-and-white picture is transmitted. However, this video signal is much wider than an audio signal because the amount of information to be transmitted for a picture is much greater.

Now, color television transmissions rely on three primary colors —red, blue and green. By using these three primary colors, all of the color information in any scene can be recreated.

The camera for color transmission contains tubes for the three colors; each "picks up" only its primary color. In addition to the luminance (light) information required in a black-and-white picture, the chrominance (color) information from these tubes must also be transmitted.

The transmission system needs to be compatible. If only a black-and-white picture is being transmitted, it must be reproduced on a color television receiver. Also, color transmissions must be reproduced on black-and-white television receivers.

In the color camera tubes, the electron beam is swept across each tube to capture the intensity of each primary color. This electrical intensity information is transmitted to the receiving picture tube on which it will be displayed.

If the reader looks at the face of a color picture tube while the set is receiving a color picture, he will see that the tube is made up of a triad of red, blue and green dots. The video signal received by the picture tube from a color camera is used to activate the respective color dot in each triad.

In a picture tube, one technique to reproduce the received color picture is to sweep three electron beams across the picture tube. Each beam activates only its respective color in proportion to the intensity of the original color. This must be done in a very precise manner to provide accurate color detail.

SCANNING AND SYNCHRONIZATION

The electron beam must be moved across the face of the camera and picture tubes in a very precise and coordinated manner. The moving or sweeping process is called scanning.

The beam of electrons move across the face of the camera and picture tubes from left to right and from top to bottom. The scanning takes place line by line. This is called the horizontal scanning or sweep process. In the U.S. the standard is 525 lines for horizontal scanning.

The number of horizontal lines helps to define the amount of picture detail that can be transmitted and received. In the U.S. each picture is actually scanned twice. The first time the odd lines are scanned and the second time the even lines of the same scene are scanned. This is called interlaced scanning and is done to reduce picture flicker. So, it takes two complete scanning fields to produce one frame, the complete picture (Figure 7.2).

The scanning process takes place at a rapid rate. Thirty pictures are scanned per second which gives 15,750 lines per second (30 frames per second times 525 lines per frame equals 15,750). In a color system, the figures are slightly less.

When the electron beam reaches the right side of the screen, it moves quickly back to the left side of the screen to start the scanning process for the next line. During the movement back to the left side, the beam is extinguished to avoid generating retrace lines.

When the beam returns to the left side of the screen, the scanning process for the next line begins at a lower point on the screen. This downward vertical movement takes place every time a new line is to be started. It is similar to starting a new line of text slightly below the previous line on a printed page.

The horizontal scanning process does not take place in a straight line across the screen. Rather the electron beam moves from left to right at a slightly downward angle.

When the last line has been scanned across the bottom of the tube, the horizontal scanning process starts again at the top of the tube. The electron beam is turned off during the vertical retrace process, and the horizontal scanning process must start at the proper location at the top of the camera and picture tube depending on whether the odd or even lines are to be scanned next.

It is during this process that the video information is being detected at the camera tube and reproduced at the receiving picture tube. Electronic circuits are required in both the television camera and the television receiver to produce the scanning action.

The scanning process at the camera tube must be properly synchronized with the scanning process at the picture tube for the video signal to be properly displayed. Pulse information is sent along with the analog video information to keep the camera tube and receiving picture tube in synchronization.

There are five basic synchronizing pulses: the horizontal-sync pulse,

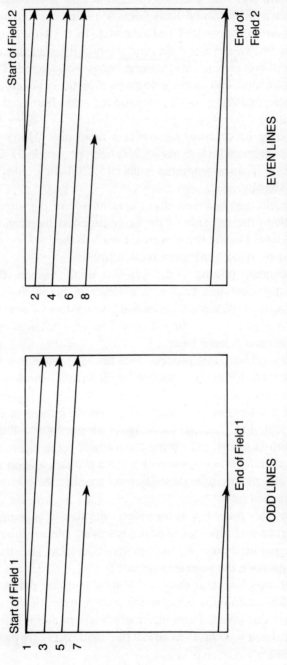

Figure 7.2. With interlaced scanning, each picture is scanned twice. The first time the odd lines are scanned, and the second time the even lines are scanned.

the horizontal-blanking pulse, the vertical-sync pulse, the vertical-blanking pulse, and the equalizing pulses.

Horizontal-sync pulses are used to keep the horizontal scanning of the camera and picture tube synchronized. The *horizontal-blanking pulse* turns off the electron beam when it is being moved back to the left side of the screen. The pulses are transmitted after each line of video. These pulses rise above the highest levels of the normal video signal and thus cause the electron beam to be extinguished during the length of the blanking pulse. This permits the electron beam to move back to the left side of the screen and not be seen during the retrace operation.

On top of the horizontal blanking pulse are the horizontal-sync pulse and a color burst signal which is an eight-cycle analog synchronization signal used when color transmission is taking place (Figure 7.3).

The *vertical-sync pulses* synchronize the vertical motion of the electron beam.

The *vertical-blanking pulse* turns off the electron beam for a vertical retrace from the bottom to the top of the screen. This pulse is rather long compared to the horizontal-blanking pulse. It takes longer for the electron beam to move from the bottom right to the top left of the screen. Riding on top of the vertical-blanking pulse are a series of vertical-sync pulses.

Also riding on the vertical-blanking pulse are the *equalizing pulses* which maintain the interlaced scanning. These pulses insure that the horizontal lines are properly spaced across the face of the screen. This includes keeping the even lines exactly between the odd lines.

There are also horizontal-sync pulses riding on the vertical-blanking pulse. The former are needed to maintain horizontal stabilization during the vertical-blanking interval. The horizontal scanning lines are inactive during this period of time since no line is being swept across the face of the tube during the vertical-blanking interval.

All of this synchronization information must be conveyed along with the video information from the camera tube to display a picture on the picture tube. Considering the speed at which the scanning process takes place, the synchronization process must be very precise.

The transmission of a color signal adds a further dimension of complexity to the transmission process. Color information is basically multiplexed onto the video carrier. This is similar to what is done when stereo is sent out on an FM radio signal. This is a greatly simplified explanation, but it conveys the idea that color information can be sent along with black-and-white information.

A final video signal includes black-and-white information, color

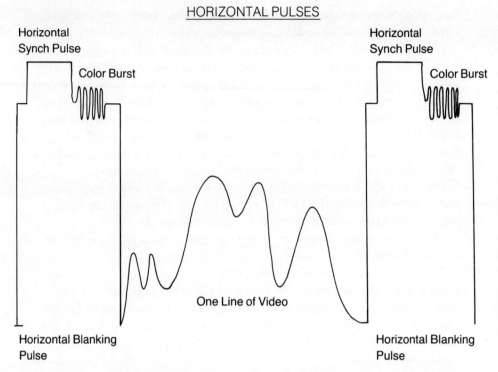

Figure 7.3. Horizontal blanking pulses are transmitted after each line of video. They contain the horizontal synch pulses and color burst signal (if color is being transmitted). _____

information, and the necessary scanning and synchronization information. This total signal is needed for the picture at the camera to be received on the receiving picture tube. Standards have been established for the transmission of this composite signal over VHF and UHF channels. These standards enable different equipment manufacturers to sell equipment which can transmit and receive a standard color or black-and-white picture.

TRANSMITTING AND RECEIVING

Once a composite video signal is created, it can be transmitted through space as a television signal. It should be understood that television signals are sent over radio waves. A television signal modulates a radio wave just as an audio signal modulates a radio wave.

In a television transmitter an oscillator generates a continuous-wave signal as in other transmitters. This signal is amplified and increased in frequency until it is at the desired transmitting frequency.

The composite video signal amplitude modulates the radio wave to transmit a television picture. However, this modulation differs somewhat from the conventional amplitude modulation. In television transmissions, negative modulation is used. In this technique, the darker scenes of the picture result in higher amplitude of the transmitted signal. The lighter scenes result in lower amplitude. An amplitude-modulated radio wave is wider—takes up more frequency spectrum—than a continuous-wave telegraph signal. An amplitude-modulated television signal is very wide compared to an amplitude-modulated radio signal used to transmit human speech.

Each television station is assigned a 6 MHz channel. A television signal is a miniature frequency spectrum of its own (Figure 7.4).

There are three components to an amplitude-modulated signal. One component is the carrier and the other two are the upper and lower sidebands. The sidebands extend out from either side of the carrier. These sidebands are needed to convey the modulation information, but they make the signal much wider.

A form of voice communications called single sideband (SSB) was mentioned in Chapter 6. In SSB, only one of the sidebands is transmitted. This is possible because the same information is contained in both sidebands. In television, a technique called vestigial sideband is used. In this technique, all of the upper sideband but only a small part of the lower sideband is transmitted. This reduces the frequency spectrum required for the transmission of a television picture over radio waves. For technical reasons, the complete elimination of the lower sideband is not practical.

TELEVISION SIGNAL

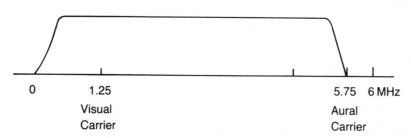

Figure 7.4. A television signal is a miniature frequency spectrum. The signal is very wide compared to a standard radio signal. _____

So, the actual transmission of a television picture is a rather straight-forward process. However, extensive equipment is needed to create the complex video signal which is presented to the transmitter for modulation and transmission.

A television receiver receives the television signal the same as a radio receiver receives radio waves (Figure 7.5). A television receiver uses the superheterodyne principle discussed in Chapter 6.

The first stage in a television receiver is an RF amplifier which amplifies the weak television signal received by the antenna. A television antenna can be a small arrangement which sits on top of the television set, a large antenna mounted on the roof of a house, or a cable system which brings the channels in from a master antenna.

Once the signal is amplified, if it sent to a mixer stage where it is combined with a local oscillator signal to produce an intermediate frequency. The IF amplifer further amplifies the television signal.

The output of the IF amplifier is sent to a video detector which detects the information contained in the carrier. Several types of information come out of the detector. The video information from the detector is sent to the video amplifier, and information related to the aural (sound) portion of the television transmission is fed to a sound IF amplifier where it is further amplified. The detector also provides all of the scanning and synchronizing instructions that is extracted from the video signal to control the movement of the electron beam across the face of the picture tube. After being amplified by the video amplifier, the video information is sent to the picture tube where it regulates the strength of the electron flow to the screen of the picture tube. This process produces the basic black-and-white picture.

From the sound IF amplifier, the signal is sent to a sound detector where the actual sound information is extracted. This signal is then sent to a sound amplifier to increase it to the level necessary to operate a loudspeaker. How the sound information is added to a television signal will be explained later in this chapter.

The synchronization pulse separator takes the video signal and separates the horizontal and vertical pulse information. These have to be separated since they each perform different functions on the electron beam. The vertical and horizontal information is used to activate circuits which sweep the electron beam across the face of the picture tube and they keep the beam synchronized with the camera tube.

The vertical and horizontal information is fed to oscillator circuits that generate the electrical signals which cause the electron beam to move

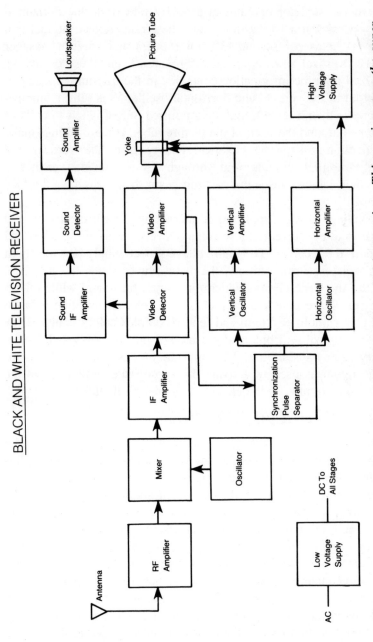

BLACK AND WHITE TELEVISION RECEIVER

Figure 7.5. A simplified diagram of a black-and-white television receiver. This receiver uses the super-heterodyne principle. To receive color signals, additional circuitry would be placed between the video amplifier and the picture tube.

horizontally across the screen and to the top of the screen after the last horizontal sweep.

The vertical oscillator operates at a 60 Hz rate while the horizontal oscillator operates at a 15,750-line rate. These rates reflect the fact that there are 60 fields per second (30 full frames) and 15,750 lines per second. The vertical and horizontal information keeps these oscillators synchronized with the information contained in the transmitted signal.

The output of the vertical and horizontal oscillators is sent to amplifiers to increase their strength, and the amplified output is fed to coils of wire wrapped around the neck of the picture tube. These windings make up a deflection yoke. The electrical energy from the vertical and horizontal amplifier circuits sent through these windings creates a magnetic field which causes the electron beam to move across the face of the screen.

A low-voltage power supply takes alternating current electricity and converts it to direct current at low voltage levels for all of the tubes and transistors in the receiver. The high-voltage power supply provides high voltage alternating current to only the picture tube.

These are the basic circuits which make up a black-and-white television receiver. To receive a color picture, the color information is taken from the video amplifier circuit and sent to complex color circuits. They develop the original red, blue and green color information which is sent with every color transmission. This information developed by the color receiving circuits is used to activate the appropriate color dots on the face of the picture tube as the electron beams scan the tube.

TELEVISION BROADCASTING

The starting point for a television broadcast is the television studio (Figure 7.6). Unlike most modern-day radio studios, television studios are usually complex and elaborate.

The camera is the heart of the television studio. There are usually multiple cameras used to focus on different aspects of a program. There is an elaborate lighting system since television cameras need a significant amount of light to generate the proper video signals. These lights are often rearranged for each program to obtain the best lighting effect.

The studio contains a number of microphones for the sound portion of the broadcast. They are high-quality microphones and are sometimes mounted overhead. Other times wireless microphones are used that contain miniature radio transmitters which send the sound signal to a nearby receiver. This eliminates the need for a visible wire from the microphone.

TELEVISION BROADCASTING

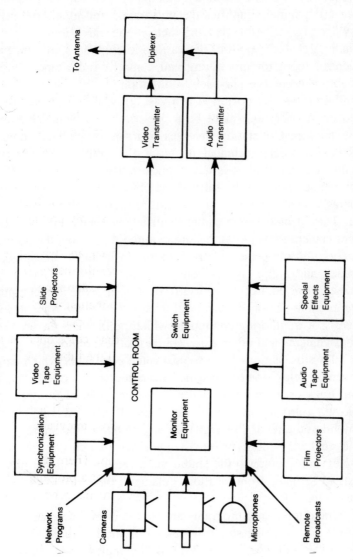

Figure 7.6. A television broadcast requires a great deal of equipment and a number of trained personnel.

The cameras generate the video signals which are sent to the studio control room for monitoring and controlling. The vertical and horizontal signals are often generated by common equipment and sent to the various cameras and other studio equipment. The use of a common synchronization signal simplifies the preparation and monitoring of the various video signals before sending them to the transmitter.

The audio signals from all of the various microphones are sent to the studio control room for monitoring and control. Audio tape machines are available if needed to playback information.

Controlling the entire operation is a vast array of personnel. While a radio broadcast operation might be a one- or two-person operation, a television broadcast operation involves many more people. Some are concerned with purely technical matters, while others are concerned with production and creative issues. Some arrange the studio sets, lights and microphones prior to the start of the broadcast, and others operate the cameras. In the studio control room are personnel who direct the program. They decide which camera will be used next and they direct the type of camera movements that are required throughout the program.

Other control room personnel are concerned with the technical quality of the video and audio signals being received from the cameras and microphones. The control room itself consists of switching equipment which permits the personnel to control what is sent to the transmitter. It also consists of monitoring equipment which permits the pictures from the various cameras and other video sources to be monitored.

Many television stations have sophisticated equipment which can be used for remote television broadcasts. This equipment is often contained in a small truck or mobile van, and a live picture can be transmitted to the studio via a private microwave radio link. Usually, a small antenna on the mobile unit sends this signal to an antenna at the studio. Some stations even have remote broadcast equipment which can transmit a remote television picture to the studio via a satellite. This permits live broadcasts to be made from locations outside of the range of the microwave radio link.

Some remote television programs are recorded on video tape recorders and then edited at the studio for playback on the studio video tape equipment. This editing process is itself a complex and sophisticated operation.

The video signal which is finally sent to the transmitter, is the result of a great deal of human effort. The transmitter and studio can be in the same building or the transmitter can be at a remote location. When the facilities are not in the same building, a wideband telephone channel or a private point-to-point microwave radio link is used to send the video signal to the transmitter. The audio information is also sent to the transmitter as a separate signal.

The video signal is sent to the modulator portion of the transmitter. One method of broadcasting the audio portion of a television broadcast is to send the audio information to a separate audio transmitter. A standard radio transmitter uses frequency modulation to transmit the audio signal.

The output of the audio transmitter is mixed with the output of the video transmitter in a diplexer and the combined signal is sent to one common antenna. This antenna then radiates a final video signal which contains both the video and audio information. In effect, the sound signal is multiplexed onto the video signal. This produces the final composite video signal which contains all of the necessary information to operate a television receiver.

The television antenna sits on top of a tall tower. The tower gets the antenna up in the air to produce the best coverage for the radiated signal. The tower itself is not part of the radiating structure, as is the case with an AM radio station tower. These towers are sometimes a thousand or more feet in height. Some have elevators for getting to the top to work on the antenna.

Tall towers are particularly helpful for UHF television. It is more difficult to generate an effective UHF signal than a VHF signal. In most cities, the first stations on the air were on VHF channels. However, cities which have no frequency assignments for the VHF channels have only UHF stations.

CABLE TELEVISION

Besides sending television signals via radio waves on VHF and UHF channels, it is also possible to send them via wire-based systems. Some of these systems will be considered in this section.

When television started to become a popular home entertainment medium, some towns were not able to receive television broadcasts. A prime example of such a situation was a small town located in a valley and surrounded by mountains. Television signals—being line-of-sight radio waves—could not be received in the valley.

One possible solution to the problem is to install an antenna on top of one of the mountains and to send the signal into the town over a very long wire. This is how cable television got its start in the U.S.

Just as human speech can be sent over wires, so also can video television signals be sent. However, the full-motion VHF and UHF television signals are too wide to be sent over a normal two-wire pair used for telephone conversations.

Television or any type of video signal is usually sent over a coaxial cable which consists of a single wire surrounded by insulating material. Around this material is wrapped a wire mesh or foil which is the ground lead for the cable. The entire cable is then surrounded with a thin layer of insulating material to prevent the outer ground conductor from being damaged.

A cable can handle a television or any video signal, and can actually carry a number of television signals through the process of multiplexing (discussed in Chapter 4). A form of frequency division multiplexing permits a coaxial cable to carry a number of television signals all at the same time.

For a cable television system which covers an entire city or town, the cable company has a central site called a head-end location where all of the television signals are received. VHF and UHF antennas are mounted on a tower to receive local and distant channels. Other channels are received via microwave relays or from satellites (Figure 7.7).

All of the television signals are placed (multiplexed) on a coaxial cable which is a main trunk line for the system. This line contains trunk amplifiers which maintain the strength of the signals over the entire length of the line.

Bridging or distribution amplifiers are connected to the main trunk line. These amplifiers are used to distribute the signals to specific locations served by the main line. Taps to the trunk line coaxial cable are made via a directional coupler which is designed to insure that the lines connected to the trunk line do not overload it. Line taps connect the branch lines from the bridging amplifiers to the various individual home subscribers. They serve to isolate the various subscribers and are designed to insure that the branch lines are not overloaded.

The coaxial cable for the cable television system is often strung on utility poles. The amplifiers are mounted in small cases along the length of the cable as required. The cable is used to distribute television signals to individual subscribers. Here, it is normally connected to a cable television converter.

Normally, the television set is tuned to channel 3 or 4. A converter unit is used to select the various channels available on the cable system.

Some cable systems carry special premium movie channels for which the subscriber must pay an extra charge. Special scrambling equipment prevents those who have not subscribed to these channels from receiving the picture. As the name implies, the picture they received is scrambled.

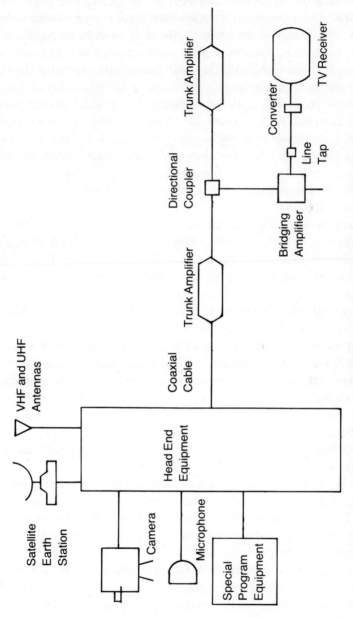

Figure 7.7. A cable television system distributes television signals via a coaxial cable.

Those who have paid for the special channels have additional descrambling equipment.

Cable television systems can also be designed to provide two-way operation. This permits information from a subscriber's home to be sent back to the head-end location. A two-way system serves many purposes. It permits burglar alarm information from a home to be monitored at the head-end site, and permits the customer to request special premium programs on a per-showing basis. The home subscriber can enter a request by entering a code on his special converter unit.

The potential to use cable television systems for other types of telecommunications certainly exists. The wide bandwidth of the coaxial cable makes it attractive for computer-related data communications. It can also be used for private television conferences. The linking of cable systems in different cities may make it attractive for long distance telecommunications.

A cable television system does not have to cover an entire city; it can be limited to a single apartment complex. Under such an arrangement, all of the antenna equipment is located at the complex. Distribution to all of the apartments is via coaxial cable. Apartment security information can also be obtained through the cable system.

Cable television can be used for other applications. Television pictures generated by security cameras in various parts of a building can be sent via coaxial cable to a central point for monitoring the building. Medical operations in one city can be transmitted via television-based cable systems to medical personnel in a conference room in the hospital or at another location across the country. Business meetings can be conducted via television. The television signals can be sent between distant cities via special wideband telephone channels, coaxial cables, or via satellite systems. This saves the cost of travel associated with business meetings.

The transmission of a standard television picture—regardless of whether it is done over cable or radio waves—is an expensive proposition. The wide bandwidth required for full-motion television simply costs a great deal to transmit. However, some telecasts do not necessarily require full-motion television. There is slow-scan television which can transmit video pictures but at much less expense. As the name implies, slow-scan systems transmit pictures at a slower rate. Typically, it might take eight seconds to scan a picture one time. However, the video signal generated by a slowscan system can be sent over a standard telephone line because it has a very narrow bandwidth compared to a standard television signal.

Slow-scan television is suitable for the transmission of pictures of documents, diagrams, etc. It can also be used to transmit pictures of people in a meeting; the system freezes the motion of the person for transmission. For many types of applications, this process is more than adequate.

Slow-scan television pictures can be sent via radio waves. Amateur radio operators regularly use slow-scan techniques to send television pictures around the world.

KEY WORDS

The reader should be familiar with the following terms in the context in which they were used in this chapter:

Amplitude Modulation

Analog Signal

Antenna

Audio

Bridging Amplifier

Broadcasting

Camera

Carrier

Chrominance

Coaxial Cable

Color

Color Burst

Compatible

Converter

Directional Coupler

Distribution Amplifier

Electrical Voltage

Electron Beam

Equalizing Pulses

Field

Fluorescent

Frame

Head-End Location

Horizontal-Blanking Pulse

Horizontal Oscillator

Horizontal-Sync

Horizontal Scanning

IF Amplifier

Interlaced Scanning

Line

Line Tap

Luminance

Magnetic Field

Microphone

Microwave

Mixer Stage

Modulation

Multiplexing

Oscillator

Photoconductive

Picture Tube

Power Supply

Primary Colors

Pulse

Radio

Retrace

RF Amplifier

Scan

Scrambling

Sidebands

Slow-Scan

Sound Detector

Standards

Sweep

Synchronization

Sync-Pulse Separator

Television

Tower

Trunk Amplifier

UHF

Vertical Oscillator

Video Tape

Vertical-Blanking Pulse

Vertical-Sync

Vestigial Sideband

VHF

Video

Video Amplifier

Video Detector

EXERCISES

1. How does scanning in a television tube generate television pictures?

2. Name the three primary colors used in a color television broadcast.

3. Explain a compatible television broadcasting system.

4. Why is synchronization necessary in a television transmission?

5. What is the purpose of interlaced scanning and how is it accomplished?

6. Name the five basic television synchronization pulses.

7. What information is contained on the vertical-blanking pulse?

8. What type of modulation is used in a television transmitter?

9. Name the basic principle used in both radio and television receivers.

10. Why is television broadcast complex?

11. How can sound be added to the video signal?

12. What are the advantages of cable television?

13. Explain slow-scan television.

8

Long Distance
Telecommunications

Prior chapters discussed radio, telephone, and computer telecommunications. The emphasis was on understanding how they operate in a local environment. This chapter discusses how telecommunications works in a long distance environment.

The term "long" is relative. In the high frequency (HF) radio range, long means hundreds and thousands of miles. In the very high frequency (VHF) range, distances of 50 or 100 miles are considered long. In this chapter, long distances are considered to be anything outside of a local metropolitan area.

This chapter builds heavily on previous chapters, particularly Chapters 4, 5 and 6. The reader should refer back to previous chapters as necessary.

TRANSMISSION MEDIUMS

Among the oldest of the long distance telecommunications transmission mediums is copper wire. To transmit telecommunications for long distances over copper wire, amplifiers and other equipment are needed to maintain the signal strength. Wire systems can run over telephone poles or can be buried in the ground. In the latter case, they are fairly secure.

To increase the capability of wire transmission systems, the multiplexing equipment discussed in Chapter 4 is used. This equipment can greatly increase the cost-effectiveness of wire-based long distance systems.

Coaxial cable (discussed in Chapter 7) is also widely used for long distance communications. The wide bandwidth makes it a good transmission medium. One cable can carry a great many telephone conversations and is well-suited for sending television programs.

Wire submarine cables connect the U.S. to Europe and other foreign countries for international telephone and telegraph communications. Many of these cables contain amplification equipment.

The latest in land-based technology is fiber optics. In this system, an optical cable is used as the transmission medium. A light signal generated by a light-emitting diode or laser is sent through this fiber. The fiber is made of sand and is about the size of a human hair.

The telecommunications transmissions are carried through an optical fiber on the light beam. An optical fiber has a very wide bandwidth and is well-suited for all types of telephone and television transmissions.

Fiber optic cables also have many other advantages. They are glass which is a much less expensive resource than copper cables. Optical fibers are light and flexible, can be easily installed, and resist deterioration. The optical fiber does not radiate electromagnetic energy so it is more secure against wire-tapping. Also, fiber optic systems do not use a conventional electrical power source and can be more easily used in hazardous areas.

Fiber optic systems are still in the process of being developed and implemented. The original applications have been for fiber optic systems on long distance routes which require a high capacity on a point-to-point basis. Economic factors will determine how quickly this new technology will replace existing technologies.

Radio waves can also be used as a long distance transmission medium over hundreds and thousands of miles on the high frequency (HF) part of the radio spectrum. These communications are possible because the radio waves are reflected off layers in the sky called the ionosphere. Via the ionosphere, radio waves can be bounced around the world.

So, the ionosphere is a sort of mirror which surrounds the earth and can reflect radio waves back to earth, but it affects radio waves differently depending on their frequency. At the very low and very high frequencies, radio waves normally pass through the ionosphere. However, at the HF part of the radio spectrum—approximately 3 to 30 MHz—the radio waves are reflected off the ionosphere. (The maximum usable frequency (MUF) is the highest frequency which is reflected by the ionosphere back to Earth.)

Transmissions at high frequencies often fade in and out. This is due to the radio waves being reflected off different parts of the ionosphere. Two different waves can arrive at the receiver and be out of phase with each other. This can cause the two waves to cancel each other out, and results in the fading of the received signal.

High frequencies are widely used for radio and teleprinter communications over great distances. They are also widely used for international radio broadcasts by almost every country in the world. The super-high frequencies are also used for long distance telecommunications via microwave radio. Radio signals at these frequencies travel in a line-of-sight path and are normally not reflected off the ionosphere. For long distance telecommunications, microwave radio systems rely on multiple repeater sites (Figure 8.1).

The end locations of a microwave radio system consist of a transmitter and receiver to send and receive telecommunications to the next site. Between the end locations are the repeater sites. They contain pairs of transmitters and receivers which receive an incoming signal and retransmit it to the next repeater. The spacing between repeaters is approximately 30 to 40 miles.

Microwave radio communications are well-suited for long distance telecommunications because of the wide bandwidths available at these frequencies. Multiplexing equipment makes possible the transmission of a large number of voice and data signals over one microwave radio signal.

Another form of long distance communications at ultra- and super-high frequencies is tropospheric scatter communications which is designed to be used over greater distances than those covered by a microwave radio system. A tropospheric system relies on radio transmissions at ultra- and super-high frequencies that are sent over the horizon back to Earth. By using sophisticated transmitting and receiving equipment, tropospheric systems can be effective over a distance of 200

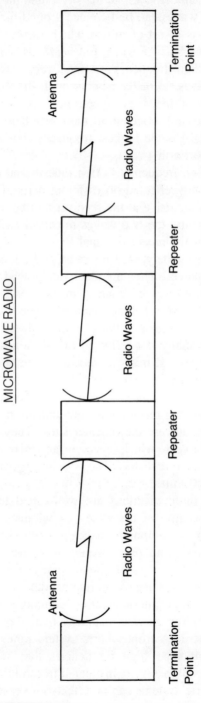

Figure 8.1. For long distance telecommunications via microwave radio, repeater sites retransmit the signal to the next site.

to 300 miles. These systems can be useful in certain applications where microwave systems are not practical, but they are not as widely used as the microwave radio systems.

The most recent form of radio communications is via satellites. Early satellite systems were passive reflectors which could reflect radio waves back to Earth; more recent systems contain their own radio equipment.

Presently, satellites are geosynchronous. They are approximately 22,300 miles above Earth and rotate at the same speed as Earth. Communications with the satellites are via up-link radio signals which are transmitted to them and down-link signals which they transmit back to Earth. Devices called transponders receive the signals, amplify them, change the frequencies, and retransmit them back to Earth. Satellites normally carry multiple transponders.

Satellites are usually in equatorial orbit. Due to the demand for space in the same approximate location over the equator, satellite congestion is starting to become a problem. So, larger satellites with increased transponder capabilities are constantly being developed to more effectively utilize the space assigned to them.

There are large earth stations near major cities in the U.S. and overseas. The stations are usually a number of miles outside of the cities to avoid problems with local radio interference. For example, earth stations for Chicago are located near Lake Geneva, Wisconsin.

One of the difficulties with using satellites for some telecommunications applications is the fact that even at the speed of light it takes approximately .27 seconds to transmit a signal one-way via a satellite. This delay is usually not a problem on television transmissions, but it can cause an echo on a telephone call. Also, for some data communications applications it can present difficulties. However, electronic equipment is constantly being developed to deal with the delay factor.

No means of long distance telecommunications is more exotic than using meteor trails as a transmission medium. Very high frequency radio signals which are normally not reflected off the ionosphere can be reflected off the ionized trails created by meteors. The large number of meteors, which are normally not seen, actually generate a fairly reliable path for some types of specialized data communications transmissions. However, this medium is not normally of interest for commercial applications.

TELEPHONE NETWORKS

A vast telephone network for long distance telecommunications has been created in the U.S. based on wire and radio transmission systems and telephone switching equipment. The Bell System first wired up the nation for long distance telephone service.

The first long distance transmission mediums were open wires on telephone poles. Coaxial cables and microwave radio systems have come to replace open wires as the long distance transmission mediums. Telephone switches have been developed to switch only long distance calls from local telephone company central office switches and from other long distance switches. What finally evolved is a five-level switching system for long distance calls (Figure 8.2).

The local telephone company central offices are at the base of this system. Further up-line are switching systems intended to only switch long distance telephone calls. This hierarchy provides alternating routing for calls, and is very helpful during periods of heavy traffic or when facilities might be damaged due to a storm.

Microwave radio systems are the backbone for the transmission of calls between the long distance telephone switches in this system. Coaxial cable and satellites are also appropriate. Fiber optic cables are being added on certain routes.

There is also a great deal of multiplex, amplification and other equipment within this long distance network. The introduction of computer-controlled long distance switches has gone a long way toward making this network more efficient and flexible. There is also a move toward making this network more digital rather than analog in nature.

Pricing on the AT&T long distance telephone network is time and distance sensitive, prime time being during the day and the lowest rates being at night and on weekends. One of the major difficulties with this or any other long distance network is that it must be built for rush hour traffic. During the off hours, a great deal of equipment sits unused.

Over a period of time, various pricing alternatives have been developed for this network, one of the most widely-known being WATS (Wide Area Telephone Service). Calls place via WATS go through this network the same as any other long distance calls. There are various WATS bands which determine how much of the U.S. can be called. The users of WATS are charged based on the number of minutes used each month. This service can provide a cost savings for organizations which place a significant amount of long distance calls.

Dedicated long distance telecommunications channels are also available. They can be connected to locations on a continuous basis for a fixed monthly charge. Large organizations often use these types of facilities for communications between major organizational plants or offices.

Another long distance offering is a foreign exchange (FX) line. (The

AT&T LONG DISTANCE SWITCHING HIERARCHY

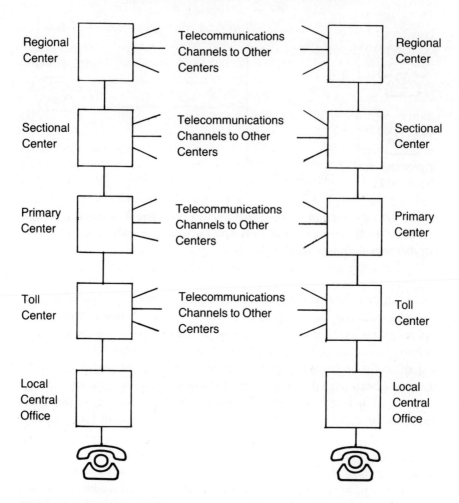

Figure 8.2. The AT&T long distance telephone network utilizes a five-level switching hierarchy. This was the original U.S. long distance network. _____

telephone exchange codes were discussed in Chapter 4.) Normally, an exchange code is assigned to the users of a specific local telephone company central office. However, by terminating an exchange code at a distant location, it becomes a foreign exchange code (Figure 8.3). When a user accesses a foreign exchange line, the dial tone he hears is from the distant city; calls can be dialed as if the person were actually in that city. Also, anyone in the distant city where the foreign exchange origi-

FOREIGN EXCHANGE LINE

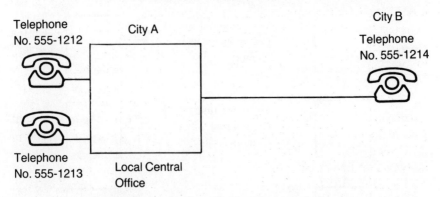

Figure 8.3. By installing a telephone number at a distant location, a foreign exchange line is created. In this example, telephone number 555-1214 from city A is installed on a telephone in city B. ——————————

nates can call the telephone number assigned to the FX line and the call will automatically be transported to wherever the FX line is terminated. There are no long distance charges to the calling party for the call.

Foreign exchange lines are priced on a fixed monthly basis similar to a dedicated telecommunications channel. However, in recent times, the trend has been to make these lines also usage sensitive. The total charge consists of a fixed cost and a variable charge based on usage. This parallels the type of pricing that is being implemented in foreign countries.

For telephone access to foreign countries, high-frequency radio systems were widely used for many years. These systems were affected by fading and other problems often encountered on HF radio. It was not until the development of voice submarine telephone cables in the 1950s that international telephone calls became more reliable. However, the cost for such calls remained high because the cost to install submarine cables is expensive and their capacity is limited.

Telephone calls to ships at sea are possible via HF radio. Gradually, satellite systems will replace HF radio for even more reliable telephone calls to ships.

Telephone calls to airplanes in the U.S. are also starting to become a reality. These systems utilize very and ultra-high radio frequencies for air-to-ground calls. Sophisticated computer-controlled earth stations make this form of telephone communications very reliable.

Until the late 1960s, long distance telephone service in the U.S. was the sole responsibility of the AT&T Long Lines Division of the Bell System. The local Bell companies and the independent telephone companies handled intrastate telecommunications.

Then, a company named Microwave Communications, Incorporated asked the Federal Communications Commission (FCC) for permission to build a microwave radio system between St. Louis and Chicago. Much to the amazement of everyone in the telecommunications industry, MCI eventually gained permission to build this system.

No one organization has a monopoly on the ability to engineer, install and maintain telecommunications equipment. This equipment—even in the 1960s—was available from a number of vendors who served the independent telephone industry and overseas customers.

Gradually, MCI and other companies built nation-wide microwave radio systems for long distance telecommunications. They moved from providing data communications to providing long distance telephone service. All of this took place at great legal expense to everyone involved since long distance telephone service was still a Bell System monopoly.

To provide routing for long distance telephone calls, these new carriers—who came to be called specialized common carriers or other common carriers (OCCs)—installed their own telephone switches in major cities in the U.S. This equipment can route a long distance telephone call to a distant city via the carriers' private microwave radio systems. In distant cities, calls still have to be completed via local telephone company central offices (Figure 8.4).

Basically, these carriers have a large number of foreign exchange lines from different cities terminated in their various switches. For locations which cannot be reached directly by the vendor's own private microwave radio systems, these switches eventually had access to the AT&T long distance network.

Sometimes, the long distance connections were established via satellite circuits. The cost for satellite channels was often less expensive than building a microwave link.

Other carriers came into existence to provide long distance telephone service. Some did not have their own long distance private microwave radio systems; they simply resold the long distance services of other vendors, including AT&T WATS. This could often be done at a profit because the carriers took low-volume users and combined their needs to get volume pricing on long distance services like WATS. These vendors came to be called resellers since they basically resold long distance services.

Even a hotel could become a long distance telephone carrier. A hotel

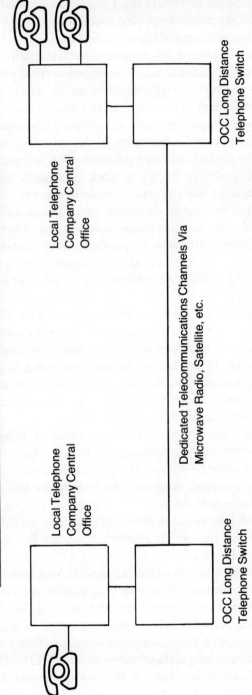

LONG DISTANCE TELECOMMUNICATIONS VIA OTHER COMMON CARRIERS

Local Telephone
Company Central
Office

OCC Long Distance
Telephone Switch

Dedicated Telecommunications Channels Via
Microwave Radio, Satellite, etc.

Local Telephone
Company Central
Office

OCC Long Distance
Telephone Switch

Figure 8.4. Other common carriers (OCCs) often establish their long distance connections via private microwave radio systems, satellite systems, etc. However, the calls still go through the local telephone company central offices.

could use its telephone system to route calls over special long distance lines. A computer printout from the telephone switch would provide immediate information on billing for guests' long distance telephone calls. Some hotels could offer guests a discount and still make money.

One of the difficulties in using most of the alternative long distance carriers was the number of digits needed to make a call. Normally, the calling party would first dial a local telephone number to access the carrier's long distance telephone switch and then enter an authorization code before dialing the call. However, as part of the divestiture of the Bell System, these other common carriers (OCCs) would have equal access to the local telephone company central offices. This means that when a customer dials the digit 1 for a long distance call, the call can be routed to long distance carriers besides AT&T. This is intended to place all of the long distance telephone carriers on an equal footing and to make the long distance telephone business truly competitive.

DATA COMMUNICATIONS

Communicating with computers—data communications—was discussed in Chapter 5. Many of the techniques used for local data communications are used for long distance data communications.

Long distance data communications networks are frequently developed through dial-up long distance telephone networks. In its most basic form, a computer terminal can be equipped with a modem and a computer can be accessed through the direct dial telephone network. The computer could also call the terminal through the same network. Many long distance data communication networks are based on just this simple type of operation.

However, cost-saving alternatives are also widely used for dial-up long distance data communications. Often, they are the same alternatives used for long distance voice communications. One widely-used alternative for data communications is WATS discussed in the previous section.

In some long distance data communication networks, the central computer calls (polls) the remote terminals on a regular basis, often via WATS or some other cost-saving service. Another approach is to have the terminal users call in to the computer on an INWATS line only when they have a need to communicate with the computer. This approach permits a small terminal to be taken to a customer's offices and calls made to a computer without placing a long distance charge on the customer's telephone bill.

Another technique is to send traffic between the terminal and the computer at night when the rates are lower. Even if not all of the traffic can be sent at night, at least some of it might be suitable for nighttime transmissions.

There are often some concerns regarding security when using dial-up long distance networks for data communications. Anyone can randomly dial-up local and long distance numbers looking for access to computer systems. To deal with this, modems with security features are rapidly being developed.

One approach is in the use of modems at the computer site which do not automatically connect an incoming call to the computer. Rather, they wait for the caller to enter the proper authorization code. The modem then disconnects the call and calls the terminal at its assigned telephone number. When the terminal answers, the call is completed to the computer. These new security technologies will become increasingly important as more organizations come to rely on the dial-up telephone network for data communications.

Dedicated telecommunications channels were discussed in Chapter 5. Such channels are also widely used for long distance data communications. The application, traffic volumes, etc. all help to determine when and if dedicated telecommunication channels are needed. The channels can be point-to-point, between the computer and one specific terminal location. Another approach is the use of multidrop dedicated channels wherein the line that leaves the central computer site goes to a number of terminal locations (Figure 8.5). This technique, when it is technically feasible, can provide a significant cost savings.

On a multidrop channel, the central computer serves as the control point for activity on the channel. The computer calls every terminal location on the channel and provides each a chance to communicate with the computer. When a terminal wishes to do so, it must wait until it is polled by the computer. However, polling takes place at such a rapid rate that users are not normally aware that the channel is being shared. If the multidrop channel becomes overloaded, users then experience delays.

Multiplexing equipment (described in Chapter 4) is also widely used on dedicated telecommunications channels to reduce data communications costs. This equipment is specifically designed for data communications, and is usually some form of time division multiplexing.

The foreign exchange lines discussed in the previous section can also be used with dial-up data communications applications. An FX line can give terminal users dial-up access to a remote computer but only one user can use the line at a time.

MULTIDROP TELECOMMUNICATIONS CHANNEL

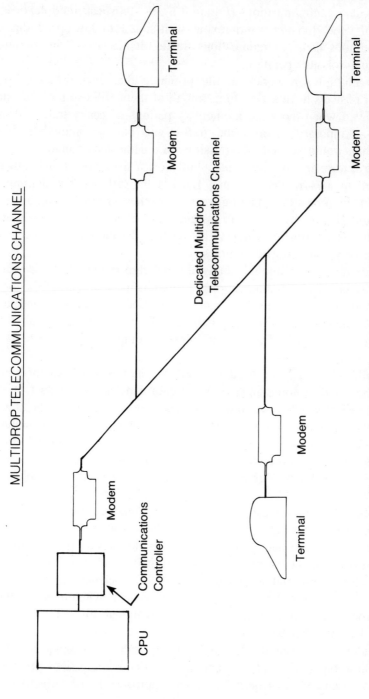

Figure 8.5. *A multidrop dedicated telecommunications channel can connect a number of terminals to a central computer.*

An alternative arrangement is to use a statistical multiplexor for dial-up data communications (Figure 8.6). A statistical multiplexor is a form of time division multiplexing well-suited to low-speed dial-up asynchronous data communications traffic. It has a built-in computer which controls its operation.

This multiplexor works on the principle that even when a large number of users have access to it, not all of them will use it at the same time. Even when there are momentary periods of heavy traffic, it can buffer—temporarily store—the traffic and can accommodate more users than would normally be possible on a dedicated channel.

With a normal time division multiplexor, a time slot on it is always assigned to a particular terminal. Even if the terminal has nothing to transmit, its time slot cannot be used by another terminal. With a statistical multiplexor, time slots are assigned to the incoming terminals only when they have traffic to send. This enables the multiplexor to accommodate very heavy traffic volumes.

All digital data communications channels are available for dedicated long distance data communications. These channels are part of the move toward all-digital systems.They can also be used in multidrop configurations. Some of these all-digital channels offer very wide bandwidths for point-to-point traffic. Special multiplexing equipment is often used on these channels.

Satellites can also be used for long distance data communications. The type of data communications protocol can have an impact on the effectiveness of data communications via satellite channels. The Binary Synchronous Communications (BSC) protocol discussed in Chapter 5 sends data one block at a time. An acknowedgment is sent back to the sending location before the next block of data is transmitted. In case of an error the acknowledgment is for a retransmission of the last block of data.

In satellite communications there is a .27-second transmission factor for the transmission of a block of data, then another .27-second factor for the acknowledgment to be sent back to the transmitting location. In some cases the computer may start to "time-out" waiting for each acknowledgment, and there can be a loss of efficiency due to the time required in sending data and waiting for an acknowledgment. If there are errors and a block of data must be retransmitted, this can further add to the loss of efficiency.

Vendors are constantly developing equipment and techniques to deal with these types of problems. The new data communications protocols, HDLC (discussed in Chapter 5), are one approach to more effective data

STATISTICAL MULTIPLEXING

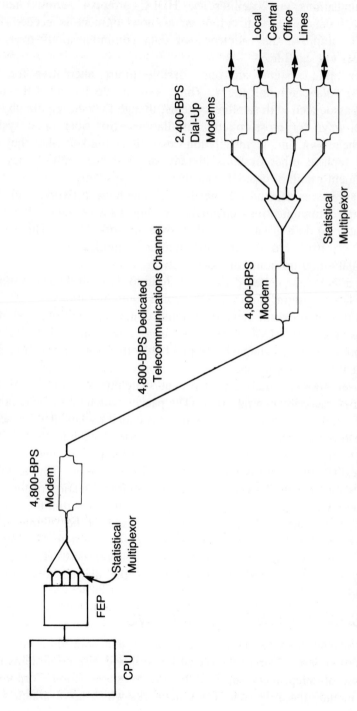

Figure 8.6. In this illustration, four 2,400-BPS dial-up channels are being sent over one dedicated 4,800-BPS telecommunications channel.

communications via satellites.The HDLC protocol permits multiple blocks of data to be sent before an acknowledgment is needed. This helps to improve the efficiency of data communications over long distances via satellite.

Fiber optic systems are one possible future alternative for long distance data communications. These systems do not have the delay factors associated with satellite systems, though they do require physical right-of-ways for cross-country installations. So, fiber optic systems have their own unique installation costs. It is unlikely that they will totally replace other systems already in existence; rather, they will supplement satellite, coaxial, and microwave systems.

Organizations that utilize the dial-up telephone networks and dedicated telecommunications channels for long distance data communications have to do a great deal of their own network design. This work is based on traffic volumes, type of equipment, applications, etc.

All-data dial-up long distance networks are now available. They utilize a technique called packet switching to transmit data communications. These systems do not handle voice communications.

In a packet network, vendors establish computer switching systems in various cities in the U.S. These systems are interconnected by dedicated telecommunications channels supplied by other vendors (Figure 8.7). The final result is a unique network for only data communications.

A user normally dials into a packet switching system via the local telephone company central office. The packet switch takes the data from the terminal and divides it into small units called packets that are sent to the destination location where they are reassembled into their original form. Each packet of data can, if desired by the packet vendor, be sent over a different transmission path to the final location. This technique permits the packet network to obtain maximum utilization of the transmission paths which connect the computer switches within the system.

Pricing on packet networks is typically based on the volume of data being transmitted rather than on the distance over which it is sent. For some data communications applications, packet networks can save money over other alternatives, including the dial-up long distance network.

MESSAGE COMMUNICATIONS

Long distance message communications are available via a number of different systems. One of the oldest but still widely-used systems is the network of teleprinters supplied by the Western Union Corporation. They include the Telex and TWX networks which are available in the U.S.

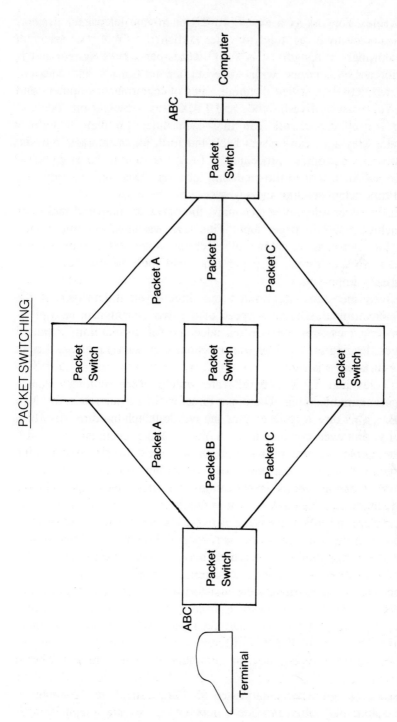

PACKET SWITCHING

Figure 8.7. Here, an original data transmission is divided into packets which are sent via three different routes. Prior to final delivery the packets are reassembled into the original transmission form.

The Telex network is a 66.67 words-per-minute teleprinter system. Telex is an acronym for "teletypewriter exchange". TWX is an acronym for "teleprinter exchange". It is a 100 words-per-minute system and is primarily a U.S. service with some service to Canada and Mexico. These two networks utilize different types of teleprinter equipment and codes; Telex uses a five-bit code and TWX uses and eight-bit code.

Users of either network can dial each other via their teleprinter terminals. Messages can be sent back and forth on an interactive basis. However, the customary procedure is for a message to be prepared in advance and then sent to the receiving location. This helps to eliminate wasted time when sending messages.

With the older teleprinter terminals, the operators prepared messages by punching holes in paper tape. This tape was then fed into a tape reader for transmission. Now, all-electronic teleprinter terminals use computer storage instead of paper tape, and message preparation has been greatly improved.

Received messages are printed out directly on the printer of the teleprinter terminal. The slow speed of the two systems can be a problem on long messages but is often adequate for normal administrative messages. Pricing for message transmissions is based on message length and the distance it is sent.

The Telex and TWX networks are widely used for long distance message communications. There is a directory of subscribers to the two networks. This directory resembles the public telephone directory for a large city, and even contains its own Yellow Pages section.

Most people are unfamiliar with these two networks because the equipment for message transmissions is often buried in the back offices of an organization. Many organizations use these networks but their employees are not even aware of that fact.

The Telex and TWX message networks are today compatible with each other through a large computer system (Figure 8.8). This system handles the compatibility differences between the two networks. This type of operation, where the messages are transmitted between two different networks, is called store-and-forward message switching.

The computer takes a message from a terminal on one network, changes the code and speed, and then retransmits it onto the other network. The users of the two different networks cannot communicate on an interactive basis but they can communicate on a store-and-forward basis.

Message communications are used for long distance telecommunications because they often provide a cost savings over a telephone call. Messages can be received at any time by a teleprinter terminal.

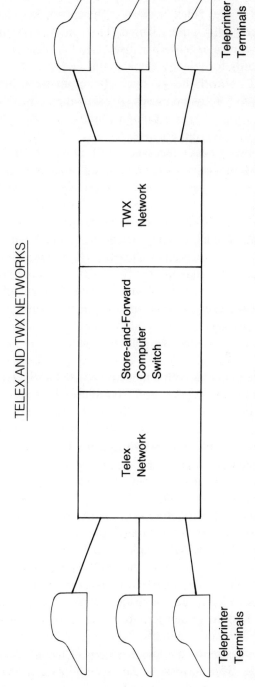

TELEX AND TWX NETWORKS

Figure 8.8. The Western Union Telex and TWX networks can communicate with each other via a store-and-forward computer switch.

The Western Union computer switch has access to submarine cables connected to Telex systems all over the world. Internationally, each country controls its own Telex network. Thanks to agencies like the International Telecommunications Union (ITU) in Switzerland, world-wide compatibility for Telex systems exists. The ITU helps countries set international standards for telecommunications.

Some organizations with heavy international message traffic have dedicated channels to foreign countries. A channel may be connected to an organization's own facility in a foreign country or it may terminate in the Telex network of a foreign country.

Some companies with heavy message traffic often establish their own computer-controlled message switching system for internal use. This system might also have access to the Telex and TWX networks. These private systems have been widely used by private companies, government agencies, and the military for many years.

One recent form of long distance message communications uses a form of mailbox to store messages. These systems are referred to as electronic mail systems, and are really a form of store-and-forward message switching which has been widely used in other applications. Users of the system are assigned individual electronic mailboxes. Anyone who is aware of the mailbox address and identification code can leave messages in it. When the user calls his mailbox, the messages can be retrieved.

Often, personal computers with a modem are used as the terminals for sending and receiving messages to and from these electronic mailboxes. This means that individuals can directly send and receive their own messages. They do not have to go through operators who prepare messages for the Telex and TWX networks, and this helps to reduce the time involved in sending and receiving messages. Also confidential material can be sent more easily when individuals have direct control over their own messages.

Facsimile machines offer another type of message communications. These machines scan documents for transmission. The scanned material is broken down into electrical information which can be transmitted over the dial-up long distance telephone network. The information to be transmitted is much less than what is involved in a television picture; rather, it resembles a slow-scan television signal.

Facsimile transmissions do not require material to be retyped. This is particularly valuable when contracts, legal documents, etc. are to be transmitted. Also, facsimile equipment is easy to use and can work on an unattended basis. Even handwritten messages can be transmitted.

Some long distance facsimile networks have been established, but most facsimile transmissions go over voice telephone networks. Again, it is a case of having a sufficient traffic volume to justify a separate facsimile network. The reality is that most people prefer telephone calls over long distance message communications.

The term "voice mail" is often used to describe systems which store-and-forward telephone calls. These systems are a great deal more sophisticated than a simple telephone answering machine. Voice mail systems are complex electronic devices that digitize human speech for storage and retransmission.

The technique used in voice mail systems is somewhat similar to electronic mail in that users have their own mailboxes for the storage of voice messages. The users of these systems can leave voice messages in mailboxes and can also retrieve messages in their own mailboxes. Typically, a user of a voice mail system uses a telephone with a tone pad to access the system. The pad is used to instruct the system regarding where messages are to be delivered. To retrieve messages, users simply call the system and enter codes to access their individual mailboxes.

The original applications for voice mail systems have been for local service within a building or a city, but they will expand into long distance operations.

Voice mail systems are sometimes provided as part of an organization's telephone system. Vendors provide systems to be shared by a number of different organizations and individuals. Security codes insure that privacy is retained.

LOCAL DISTRIBUTION

Traditionally, the local telephone company has served as the access point for long distance telecommunications. There are a number of practical reasons for this. One reason is that the local telephone companies already had facilities in place to reach everyone in a city. As new vendors of long distance services came into existence, they tried to utilize the local distribution facilities already in existence.

Since the divestiture of the Bell System, local distribution has started to take on new significance. Many long distance carriers would like to have more direct control over the end-to-end delivery of their services. In some cases, they would like to bypass the local telephone company central offices and their associated wires and cables.

The issue of bypass is of serious concern to local telephone companies. It will have a serious impact on their revenues.

One alternative approach being taken in some cities is the development of a teleport. It can be viewed as an alternative to the local telephone company central office for access to long distance telecommunications services.

A teleport has access to different long distance services via satellites, microwave, radio, coaxial cable, etc. A teleport offers users access to a wide variety of long distance services for data, voice, television and message communications. Availability is on an as-needed basis. A teleport can have its own switch to select the best route for each customer's call. The possibilities are unlimited.

However, there is the question of local access to a teleport or any other alternative long distance telecommunications service without using the facilities of the local telephone company. One technique is to use small local microwave systems to connect customers directly to a teleport and other long distance service. Small intracity microwave systems have started to become more economically viable.

However, there may be limits to the use of local microwave systems within a city, considering the potential interference problems. Being line-of-sight systems, they need a clear path from the antenna of a customer to a teleport or other central site. In cities with tall buildings, this poses serious problems.

Another alternative for local distribution is the installation of fiber optic systems within a city. Such systems could offer the type of bandwidth needed for telephone, television, data and message communications. However, this would require gaining access to telephone poles and conduits already being used by the local telephone company.

Cable television systems also may be used for local distribution. Since these systems already exist in most cities, there would not be the initial problems associated with other alternatives, and they typically have very wide bandwidths. However, cable systems have been created to deal with home entertainment. The transmission of other types of telephone and data communications would require the local cable companies to learn a great deal about other types of telecommunications.

Some users may find it economically viable to directly access a satellite system from an antenna at their own facility. The cost of earth stations continues to decrease and the antennas continue to be reduced in size as satellites move to even higher radio frequencies. However, this would not solve the problem of local distribution for other than access to satellite systems.

There are other possible alternatives for one-way distribution from a central site to locations within a city. One form of one-way distribution could take place via a channel multiplexed onto a local FM radio signal. This was discussed in Chapter 6.

The potential also exists for limited data transmissions on television broadcast signals during the vertical-blanking interval. This would probably be suitable for only very specialized applications.

The local distribution issue should more fully acquaint the reader with the political and economic issues involved in many telecommunications matters. It is not just a question of what is technically possible but also of what is economically and politically feasible.

For example, should cable television companies be permitted to serve as a means of bypassing the local telephone company central offices? Would the local cable company even want to be in this new line of business?

If bypass by any means is permitted, would local telephone subscribers be forced to pay more for service to make up for revenues lost by local telephone companies? The questions are literally endless and do not have nice neat technical answers.

KEY WORDS

The reader should be familiar with the following terms in the context in which they were used in this chapter:

Amplification

BSC

Bypass

Cable

Coaxial Cable

Data Communications

Dedicated Channel

Delay

Dial-Up

Down-Link

Earth Station

Echo

Electronic Mail

Equal Access

Fading

Facsimile

Fiber Optics

FX

Geosynchronous

HF Radio

HDLC

Ionosphere

ITU

Local Distribution

Mailbox

Message Communications

Message Switching

Meteor Trails

Microwave Radio

MUF

Multidrop

Multiplexing

OCC

Packet Switching

Polling

Protocol

Radio Waves

Satellite

Statistical Multiplexor

Submarine Cable

Sunspot Cycle

Telephone Network

Telephone Switch

Teleport

Teleprinter

Telex

Time Division Multiplexing

Transmission Mediums

Tropospheric Scatter System

TWX

Up-Link

VHF

Voice Mail

WATS

Wire

EXERCISES

1. How has multiplexing equipment extended the economic life of wire transmission systems?

2. Name the advantages of fiber optic cables.

3. How are HF radio waves transmitted around the world?

4. Why do geosynchronous satellites appear to remain in one place in the sky?

5. Explain the differences between WATS service and an FX line.

6. What is equal access?

7. Draw a diagram of a multidrop dedicated data communications channel.

8. Why do some data communications protocols have difficulties with satellite systems?

9. Explain packet switching.

10. Why is message communications not used more widely by organizations as an alternative to long distance telephone calls?

11. List three different types of message communications systems and explain their advantages and disadvantages.

12. What is bypass?

13. How can users access long distance telecommunications services?

14. Are decisions related to long distance telecommunications always related to just technical considerations? Explain your answer.

9

Careers in Telecommunications

TELECOMMUNICATIONS PERSONNEL
EDUCATION AND TRAINING
TELECOMMUNICATIONS JOBS
EMPLOYERS
ASSOCIATIONS AND PUBLICATIONS
KEY WORDS
EXERCISES

This chapter examines the main types of telecommunications personnel and the jobs which they perform. Also examined is how they have been educated and trained for their jobs. Telecommunications employers and professional associations and publications are also explained. This chapter will give the reader a good overview of the telecommunications field in terms of career opportunities.

This chapter will also be of value to anyone already working in the telecommunications field, since it will help to explain what others in the field do for a living. It is not unusual to sit in a meeting with experienced telecommunications personnel and realize that there is a lack of clear understanding regarding everyone's job function.

TELECOMMUNICATIONS PERSONNEL

There are quite a number of different types of telecommunications personnel (Table 9.1). Among them are *telecommunications techni-*

Table 9.1. Telecommunications personnel (partial listing). _____

Technicians
Engineers
Scientists
Computer programmers
Analysts
Designers
Planners
Consultants
Marketers
Salespersons
Business managers
Entrepreneurs
Lawyers

cians. They are usually hands-on people who work directly with equipment. Technicians have a "feel" for equipment. They can build it, install it, repair it, etc. They also have the ability to work with complex systems made up of different types of equipment.

Telecommunications technicians usually have a significant amount of theoretical knowledge about telecommunications, yet they usually need to physically work with equipment to relate theory to practice. Regardless of what a book says, technicians know how the equipment works in the real world.

Telecommunications engineers are usually more removed from direct hands-on involvement. They are usually more mathematically-oriented in their approach to equipment and systems. In the U.S., registered professional engineers are licensed by each state. However, many engineers who work in the telecommunications field are not licensed professional engineers and often may not even have a college degree.

So, telecommunications engineering personnel must be considered more in terms of the work they actually perform. They often work with mathematics, charts, graphs, tables and abstractions and develop plans for work to be performed by technicians.

One category of telecommunications engineer—the *field engineer*—is a cross between a technician and a more traditional engineer. Field engineers often work closely with telecommunications equipment on a hands-on basis, and usually have a sophisticated technical background in telecommunications.

A new category is the *engineering technologist*. Such persons usually have a college degree in engineering technology which combines theoretical and equipment training.

Scientists involved in telecommunications are normally involved in some specific area of the field and on fairly abstract problems. They often work in research laboratories. *Telecommunications scientists* are often involved in research and development, product development, etc. They perform experiments and make calculations.

Computer programmers are a fairly recent entry to the field of telecommunications. Many telecommunications systems are controlled by computers, and they require programmers to develop the software for these systems. Programmers are relatively unknown outside the industry because so much of their work is done behind the scenes. Also, it is abstract work which doesn't make for easy reading or small talk at parties.

Typically, it is easier to develop telecommunications equipment than the programs which are often necessary to make the equipment work. At this stage, programming for telecommunications equipment and systems is still as much of an art as it is a science.

Telecommunications analysts are interested in systems. Their interests often cross over traditional technical specialties and boundaries. They may work with end-users of telecommunications equipment and systems to help them deal with their needs and problems.

Designers create new equipment and systems from components.

Telecommunications planners look to the future. They plan for new products, networks, systems, etc. Their work is rather abstract since their planning may involve telecommunications equipment which may not yet even be in existence. They may also be concerned with telecommunications needs which are only starting to evolve. Planners need to understand many different aspects of telecommunications equipment and systems.

Telecommunications consultants work on a wide range of activities. They can be specialists in specific areas of telecommunications or generalists who cover wide areas. For example, they may specialize in designing electronic circuits or computer programs, or in understanding telecommunications technology to solve specific business problems.

Telecommunications marketing personnel are concerned with understanding the market for products and services. The most technically sophisticated telecommunications product or service is of no real value if no one wants it. For instance, the video telephone was a great product, yet it did not take off in the marketplace. It is often difficult to predict what people will buy, regardless of the best marketing efforts.

Telecommunications sales personnel sell the product or service. Like the telecommunications technician, the salesperson's job is very much a hands-on type of job. Sales personnel deal directly with customers in getting them to buy equipment and services.

Telecommunications business personnel are responsible for the overall operation of the business. They may be specialists in some specific area like engineering or marketing, or they may be general managers who oversee multiple functions. They are concerned with managing people and with making money. The latter has not always been easy in the field of telecommunications. Some companies have failed to succeed in this field. Some areas of telecommunications are very capital-intensive and require a great deal of financing, long distance telephone service being one example. So, it takes capable business personnel to make a profit in this industry.

Telecommunications entrepreneurs have somewhat replaced the inventors of the past. Today, inventions in this field are often products of large research organizations, and often entrepreneurs take these products and turn them into money-making products and services. Entrepreneurs often like to work alone, have a good imagination, creativity, and a sense of showmanship. They have the ability to not only understand the technical aspects of telecommunications but also the market.

The field of telecommunications has been fraught with legal battles since its inception. Some *lawyers* have become specialists in the field of telecommunications. This requires not only legal expertise but a significant amount of technical knowledge.

EDUCATION AND TRAINING

Telecommunications personnel are educated and trained in many ways. It is fascinating to understand their educational backgrounds.

The military services have been a source of education and training for many of the personnel. The military services conduct many courses and schools related to telecommunications. Some of these courses train enlisted personnel as technicians, while other courses train officers to be managers of telecommunications systems. These courses can run from weeks to months.

The U.S. Army Signal Center at Fort Gordon in Georgia has over 5,000 personnel involved in training related to the field of telecommunications. The other military services conduct their own schools.

Since most people do not make the military a career, those who leave the military services often enter the civilian telecommunications field.

Some continue their civilian education based on their exposure to telecommunications in the military.

Amateur radio has also been a training ground for telecommunications personnel; it is good for providing hands-on exposure to equipment. Amateur radio operators know all too well that equipment often works much differently in the real world than textbooks indicate it should.

Some telecommunications personnel are self-taught. In an age of formal schooling it is difficult to appreciate that some people have simply taught themselves telecommunications from library books. These people have often had some additional training through amateur radio or the military services, yet much of their real education was obtained at public libraries.

Civilian technical schools also exist to teach telecommunications. To some degree, they are being replaced with two-year college degree programs.

Independent self-study courses have also been widely used by telecommunications personnel as a method of increasing their technical knowledge (Table 9.2). This has been a hidden training area best known to people already in the field. Self-study courses meet the needs of many people, including those who work shifts or who travel.

One self-study school which has been in existence for many years and has continued to progress with the times is the Cleveland Institute of Electronics, Cleveland, Ohio. Started originally with an orientation toward the field of radio and TV broadcasting, it has expanded its courses over the years. Today, its courses include all aspects of telecommunications, including computers. The school even offers engineering-level courses and a two-year Associate Degree.

Many private companies conduct their own internal telecommunications courses. Some have even built their own schools to train their personnel. The schools often rival colleges in technical sophistication.

Table 9.2. Telecommunications courses through independent self-study (partial listing).

Cleveland Institute of Electronics	Cleveland, OH
Grantham College of Engineering	Los Alamitos, CA
Heath/Zenith Electronics	St. Joseph, MI
International Correspondence School	Scranton, PA
National Technical Schools	Los Angeles, CA
NRI School of Electronics	Washington, DC

For years, the Bell System was a leader in conducting internal training courses. Many of the people it trained ultimately left the Bell System, and smaller telecommunications companies were able to benefit greatly by hiring these well-trained personnel.

Every day in the U.S., thousands of people are taking telecommunications seminars. These short courses are intended for various levels of technical sophistication (Table 9.3). Some are designed for entry level personnel while others are for more experienced people. Many companies regularly send their telecommunications personnel to short courses and seminars. Some people have literally learned the telecommunications business from such courses, along with self-study and on-the-job training.

Recently there has been a significant increase in two-year Associate Degree college programs to train telecommunications personnel. Sometimes this training is in electronics with an orientation to telecommunications. Associate Degree programs teach fundamentals, including the mathematics involved in electronic circuits. There is also heavy involvement with hands-on use of equipment and practical experimentation. The two-year programs have brought some standardization to training, compared to proprietary schools which often differ greatly in the types of training they offer. The programs are often an alternative for people who are not oriented toward a four-year degree.

Four-year Bachelor's Degree programs have been in existence for many years to provide college-trained engineers. Typically, the degree pursued by students interested in telecommunications has been in the

Table 9.3. Telecommunications training material and seminars (partial listing).

abc TeleTraining	Geneva, IL
American Management Association	New York, NY
Auerbach Publishers	Pennsauken, NJ
BCR Enterprises	Hinsdale, IL
Center for Advanced Professional Education	Santa Ana, CA
Datapro Research Corporation	Delran, NJ
Data Sources	Chicago, IL
Electronic Writers and Editors	New Hyde Park, NY
Systems Technology Forum	Burke, VA
TeleStrategies	McLean, VA
The American Institute	Madison, NJ
The Sander Group	Severna Park, MD

field of electrical engineering. Some colleges and universities also offer programs at both the undergraduate and graduate level in telecommunications (Table 9.4). Some of these programs are engineering-oriented, while others are more systems-oriented.

There is a need for students with hands-on training who are educated at the Bachelor's level. This is fulfilled by a degree called the Bachelor of Science in Engineering Technology. It is a four-year program. This new program has started to take hold, and its graduates are finding a demand for their training. Capitol Institute of Technology in Laurel, MD offers an engineering technology degree with a major in telecommunications to provide its students with more specialized training.

Also at the undergraduate level are college programs that train students for the field of radio and TV broadcasting. They are not engineering programs, and are often offered by liberal arts departments. However, they often have significant technical content. Youngstown State University in Youngstown, Ohio is one school that offers such a program. The school also has its own radio station and television studios.

So, at the undergraduate level there are a number of degree programs related to telecommunications. Yet, it is often easier for a university to develop a new degree program on the graduate level than to change the traditional undergraduate degree programs.

The University of Colorado in Boulder, CO started one of the first

Table 9.4. Telecommunications programs in colleges and universities at the Bachelors level and higher (partial listing).

Capitol Institute of Technology	Laurel, MD
DeVry Institute of Technology	Evanston, IL
George Washington University	Washington, DC
Golden Gate University	San Francisco, CA
Michigan State University	East Lansing, MI
Mundelin College	Chicago, IL
New York University	New York, NY
Ohio University	Athens, OH
Polytechnic Institute of New York	Brooklyn, NY
Southern Methodist University	Dallas, TX
Southern Technical Institute	Marietta, GA
University of Colorado	Boulder, CO
University of Pittsburgh	Pittsburgh, PA
University of Southern California	Los Angeles, CA
Youngstown State University	Youngstown, OH

Master's Degree programs in telecommunications. The courses are taught by both technical and nontechnical faculty members. The program is intended to provide students with a broad background in the field of telecommunications. Its graduates have gone on to positions with companies that produce telecommunications equipment and services and organizations which use telecommunications services.

Many engineers go on to graduate training at the Master's or Doctoral level. This type of graduate education has been in existence for many years. The stress at the graduate school level is on theory and research. Scientists who work in telecommunications are typically educated at one of these levels.

Lawyers who work in telecommunications receive the standard law school education after completion of undergraduate programs at the Bachelor's level. Their undergraduate education can be in any number of areas.

Business personnel who work in telecommunications often have undergraduate degrees in business, finance, economics, etc. They may also have a graduate degree, the Master of Business Administration being a widely-held degree.

TELECOMMUNICATIONS JOBS

One confusing aspect about the telecommunications field is that often people with very different types of backgrounds perform the same job or work in the same functional area (Table 9.5). This often confuses even people within the industry. For example, research and development work is widely done within this industry, yet people with varying backgrounds are involved in this type work.

Obviously, it is an area that has scientists and engineers, and also has technicians who are often involved in working with equipment, building prototypes, etc. Some have Associate Degrees while others have a background in military electronics. Technical writers with degrees in English may be involved in R&D. They may be involved in converting technical information into material which can be understood by nontechnical personnel.

Product development is another area which can involve many different types of telecommunication personnel, including engineers and sales and marketing people. It takes a variety of talents to develop new telecommunications products.

Telecommunications equipment must be produced as reliably and cost-effectively as possible. Manufacturing personnel are constantly searching for new methods to produce equipment. In some companies,

Table 9.5. Telecommunications jobs (partial listing). _____

> Research and development
> Product development
> Manufacturing
> Technical writing
> Training
> Selling
> Consulting
> Planning
> Installation and repair
> Managing

telecommunications is being used to link designers and other manufacturing personnel directly to the production line. Often, data communications systems are used to coordinate the flow of raw materials to the assembly line. So, new jobs involving telecommunications are constantly being added to manufacturing operations.

Also in the area of telecommunications manufacturing are writing jobs wherein people write user manuals, repair manuals, etc. These people take technical matter and relate it in less technical terms. Personnel in this area have engineering backgrounds, liberal arts degrees, field experience as technicians, etc. Turning technical material into something that can be understood by less technically-oriented users is not an easy task, yet it is often critical to the ultimate success of products in the marketplace.

Training related to telecommunications is a never-ending task. Sales personnel have to be trained on how to sell a new product, engineers have to be instructed on how the product can be used, users have to be instructed on how to operate telecommunications equipment, and so on.

Once a product is created it must be sold. Selling involves a number of different types of personnel. The people who do the actual selling of telecommunications equipment and services may have engineering degrees or varied business experience.

Selling is one field where results can be easily measured: Did the salesperson make his quota? Sometimes, technical personnel find it difficult to relate the technical aspects of a product—its features—to the needs of customers, and a lack of technical knowledge makes it difficult for a salesperson to understand how a product can be useful to a customer.

Selling telecommunications products can be a real challenge. The reader has only to look through the classified section of any major newspaper to see the crying demand for sales personnel.

To help deal with a shortage of qualified personnel, many organizations have large support staffs of technical personnel who can assist the salespeople. These staffs are comprised of engineers, technicians, etc. who assist the salesperson in dealing with technical issues related to equipment and services and the customer's needs.

By providing salespeople with sophisticated technical assistance, the salesperson can concentrate on the selling aspects of his or her job. This team approach enables selling functions in any company to be much more effective.

Telecommunications consulting is another area which attracts a variety of backgrounds. Some people with degrees in telecommunications may start out working directly in the area of telecommunications consulting. However, the more common path is for someone with practical experience in one or more areas of telecommunications to enter the field at a later age.

Consulting is often done by small firms or individuals who work alone. This means that they need not only technical experience in telecommunications but also the ability to sell their services and to manage their own businesses. People in this field have all types of backgrounds and educations. It is not usually an area which people plan to enter; rather, they often unexpectedly discover it.

Planning related to developing new telecommunications products and services and in utilizing them can again involve personnel with diverse backgrounds. Large planning operations have people with backgrounds in engineering, sales, business, service, etc. all working on the same staff. No one type of person has all the answers.

Installation and repair of telecommunications equipment is often performed by technicians or field engineering personnel. The emphasis here is not on people with just theoretical knowledge but on people who can work hands-on to get a job done. Technical competency or a lack of it is quickly apparent.

The management of telecommunications activities, like any other type of management, involves getting things done through other people. It involves understanding and working with people with different backgrounds and experiences. Some technical people find dealing with others to be a frustrating task and one that they would rather avoid. This is probably no more the case in telecommunications than in any other field.

Sometimes, an average engineer, salesperson, technician, etc. turns out to be an excellent manager or supervisor. They simply function better as overseers than as doers. In other cases, the first promotion to a management or supervisory position turns out to be a disaster. Success in this area is often difficult to predict in advance.

EMPLOYERS

There are as many different types of telecommunication employers as there are telecommunication personnel, educational backgrounds and jobs within the industry. The telecommunications industry can be broken down into major categories of employers (Table 9.6).

At the most basic level are manufacturing companies which produce electronic components, resistors, transistors, etc. The components are used in a wide variety of electronic equipment, so the need for specialized telecommunications personnel is limited. However, companies which manufacture equipment from these components have a need for specialized personnel. The companies manufacture modems, telephone switches, radio transmitters, etc. Some of this equipment might be used by other manufacturers as part of even more complex telecommunications equipment.

Telecommunications manufacturing companies have a need for various types of personnel—engineers, technicians, planners, designers, salespeople, etc. Some companies are very technically-oriented, while others are more oriented to marketing.

It is relatively easy to form a telecommunications manufacturing company. They have been started in garages and basements of homes and sometimes go on to become large operations. Some companies are in very specialized product areas and are unknown except to people in the telecommunications industry.

Some small companies sell their products through independent manufacturing representatives who represent a number of different compa-

Table 9.6. Telecommunications employers (partial listing). _____

Manufacturers
Equipment integrators
Installation companies
Retailers
Telephone industry
Broadcast industry
User organizations
Government agencies

nies. Installation and service might be provided through a third party under contract to the manufacturing company.

Large telecommunications manufacturers typically have a staff to cover everything from manufacturing to sales and service. When they need a new product line, they may simply buy up a smaller company which has the product.

Foreign manufacturing companies of telecommunications equipment are now heavily involved in the U.S. markets. Some of their equipment is even manufactured in the U.S. They are another source of telecommunications employment.

Some companies integrate equipment manufactured by other companies to produce even more complex equipment. Sometimes this equipment is sold as a new piece of equipment or as a service. For example, a building developer may integrate telephone switching equipment, satellite antennas, etc. into an office building to offer the tenants services on a shared basis. The developer will need telecommunications personnel to operate and maintain this equipment.

Equipment integrators are becoming increasingly popular because they are often able to offer new types of equipment and services. Entry to the market can often be relatively easy since the basic equipment is manufactured by other companies. However, there must be a real market for the final equipment or service for an integrator to succeed.

Companies which install and maintain telecommunications equipment are widespread. This work is often done by large companies as part of their total sales effort. This work requires the effort of technicians, engineers and other technical personnel. Support personnel to handle scheduling and management are also needed.

Some telecommunications companies specialize in the installation and maintenance work related to equipment. They may work on a contractual basis for a number of different telecommunications manufacturers. For example, there are companies which specialize in installing cable television equipment, including coaxial cable on telephone poles. They go from one town to the next doing this type of work.

Retailers of telecommunications equipment sell directly to end-users. Many are independent local operations. Two-way radio systems for automobiles and other vehicles can be sold and maintained directly by the equipment manufacturers or by local independent retailers. Both have a need for personnel who can sell, install and maintain this equipment. The Yellow Pages show the local retailers of telecommunications equipment. They may be listed under a number of different categories including data communications equipment, radio communications equipment, and telephone equipment.

Historically, one of the largest employers of telecommunications personnel has been the telephone industry. Since the deregulation of this industry, new types of telephone companies have come into existence, such as those offering long distance voice services, satellite communications, and data communications services. The range of personnel needed by these industries is wide. It includes scientists, engineers, marketing personnel, installation people, etc.

Many jobs within the telephone industry are rather unique to the needs of this industry. These involve coordination functions related to the installation of services for customers and coordination with multiple vendors. Personnel are usually trained on-the-job for many of these positions.

The radio and TV broadcasting industry has always been a source of employment for telecommunications personnel. Employment opportunities have increased with the advent of cable television and public radio and television stations.

The broadcasting industry needs personnel to operate and maintain radio and television equipment. This work is often done by technicians or field engineering personnel. Technical personnel are often called broadcasting engineers, which is sometimes confusing since the work is usually at a technician or field engineer level. Hands-on ability is what most stations need. Some larger broadcasting operations have engineering personnel involved with designing new studio systems and transmitter facilities. This is closer to the more traditional work performed by engineers.

The broadcasting industry seems glamorous. However, the reality is that broadcast personnel often work nights, weekends, and holidays. Outsiders often fail to understand this when listening to a radio station or watching a TV program.

Many large companies have their own telecommunications staffs to manage voice and data communications systems. These companies include banks, insurance firms, and manufacturers. Typically, they employ technically-oriented personnel—engineers, analysts, and technicians. These personnel are involved in analyzing the organizations's telecommunications needs, designing networks, installing equipment, etc.

The military services also employ civilian telecommunications personnel with technical backgrounds. Many government agencies including the CIA, NASA, and the GSA employ telecommunications personnel. These are Civil Service jobs with all the benefits of government employment.

ASSOCIATIONS AND PUBLICATIONS

Associations and publications tell a great deal about any field of endeavor, including telecommunications. People join telecommunications associations because of common interests. Associations do not usually cover the entire field of telecommunications, but instead concentrate on specific aspects of the industry (Table 9.7).

These associations provide their members with strength through numbers. Associations are formed for the exchange of information, discussion of common problems, lobbying activities, etc. Some associations are formed for the purpose of certifying its members.

The American Radio Relay League (ARRL) was established in the early days of radio to promote the interests of amateur radio operators. It is still the largest and best-known of the amateur radio associations. It has its own publication, *QST*, which is widely read by amateur radio operators.

The ARRL works with the FCC on matters relating to amateur radio operators. Many telecommunications personnel who hold professional jobs in the field are also amateur radio operators.

The Institute of Electrical and Electronics Engineers (IEEE) was formed through the merger of two other associations, the American Institute of Electrical Engineers and the Institute of Radio Engineers. Many of the members of the IEEE are actively involved in telecommunications work, particularly as engineers and scientists. The IEEE has numerous technical publications, some directly related to telecommunications. Local IEEE chapters serve as a meeting point for members. The IEEE also has student chapters at colleges and universities.

The Society of Broadcast Engineers is made up of technical personnel who work in the radio and TV broadcasting industry. Previously, the standard for technical employment as a technician or broadcasting engineer was the First Class Radiotelephone Operators License. As part of the deregulation of the telecommunications industry, the FCC eliminated this license and the requirements for it to operate radio and TV broadcasting equipment.

The Society of Broadcast Engineers has developed a voluntary certification program for broadcasting personnel to serve as a guide to technical proficiency since the elimination of the First Class License. The

Table 9.7. Telecommunications associations (partial listing). _____

American Radio Relay League	Newington, CT
Armed Forces Communications and Electronics Association	Burke, VA
Federal Communications Bar Association	Washington, DC
International Communictions Association	Dallas, TX
International Society of Certified Electronics Technicians	Forth Worth, TX
International Telecommunications Satellite Organization	Washington, DC
Institute of Electrical and Electronics Engineers	New York, NY
National Association of Broadcasters	Washington, DC
National Association of Radio and Telecommunications Engineers	Salem, OR
National Satellite Cable Association	Richmond, TX
Society of Broadcast Engineers	Indianapolis, IN
Society of Wireless Pioneers	Santa Rosa, CA
Tele-Communications Association	West Covina, CA
United States Telecommunications Suppliers Association	Chicago, IL
United States Telephone Association	Washington, DC

society also provides its members with information of common interest related to the field of radio and TV broadcasting.

In the Washington, DC area, lawyers and engineers who work closely with the FCC on telecommunications matters have their own associations. This is one example of a rather specialized area of telecommunications where many of the practitioners are all in the same geographic area.

Many user groups are formed to represent the interests of personnel who utilize certain types of telecommunications equipment. For example, users of certain types of telephone systems may have a group to discuss common problems and to represent their interests before vendors.

Other user groups are concerned with the general application of telecommunications within organizations. The International Communications Association (ICA) is made up of companies which have large voice and data telecommunications facilities. The ICA has its own internal publications for distribution only to its members, and represents its member companies before Congress, the FCC, etc. on matters related to telecommunications. The annual ICA convention brings the members together and gives them the opportunity to attend seminars and to examine new telecommunications equipment.

There are many other excellent telecommunications associations similar to the ICA. The TeleCommunications Association (TCA) is a large user group. It has local chapters that hold regular meetings.

The National Association of Broadcasters represents the radio and TV stations which belong to it on matters related to their common interests. It also provides its members with information related to radio and television broadcasting. Its members are radio and TV stations rather than specific individuals.

The United States Telephone Association represents the interests of telephone companies in the U.S. There are hundreds of telephone companies in the U.S.; some have been in existence since the start of the telephone industry. The association holds an annual meeting where members can attend seminars and examine new equipment.

The development of cable television, satellite communications, etc. has given birth to new associations for those interested in these new areas.

The *Encyclopedia of Associations*, available at public libraries, will help the reader to locate specific telecommunications associations. Association activities are listed in their publications.

There are a large number of telecommunications publications (Table 9.8). Some are published by associations, while others are available to anyone who wants to purchase them. Some publications are distributed on a no-charge basis to qualified telecommunications personnel.

Communications Week informs its readers of telecommunications activities related to the telephone and data communications industries. It is widely read by vendors and users.

Communications News is a monthly publication that focuses on news and technical articles related to various aspects of telecommunications. It has articles on voice and data communications, radio systems, etc., and provides excellent coverage of telecommunications conferences around the U.S.

Publications like *Telephony* are oriented to technical aspects of the telephone industry. This publication has been widely read for many

Table 9.8. Telecommunications periodical publications (partial listing).

Broadcast Engineering	Overland Park, KS
Cable Television	Englewood, CO
Communications News	Geneva, IL
CQ	Hicksville, NY
Data Communications	New York, NY
Electronics Business	Boston, MA
International Television	New York, NY
Modern Electronics	Hicksville, NY
Personal Communications	Fairfax, VA
Popular Communications	Hicksville, NY
Radio-Electronics	New York, NY
Satellite Dish	Memphis, TX
Sound and Communications	New York, NY
Telemarketing	Norwalk, CT
Telephony	Chicago, IL

years by people within the industry. Other publications, like *Data Communications,* specialize in technical issues.

Telemarketing is a publication which focuses on the interests of people who utilize the telephone for sales and marketing activities. It contains a mixture of technical and sales-oriented articles.

Radio Electronics, Modern Electronics and others feature technical articles complete with schematic diagrams. These types of publications often appeal to technicians, engineers, and hobbyists.

Public libraries have a number of reference books which list various periodical publications currently in print. No matter how specialized a reader's interest may be, there will most likely be a periodical publication available.

KEY WORDS

The reader should be familiar with the following terms in the context in which they were used in this chapter:

Amateur Radio

Analyst

ARRL

Associate Degree

Bachelor's Degree

Broadcasting

Computer Programmer

Consultant

Designer

Doctoral Degree

Engineer

Engineering Technologist

Entrepreneur

Equipment Integrator

Field Engineer

ICA

IEEE

Manager

Manufacturing

Marketing

Master's Degree

Planner

Product Development

Research and Development (R&D)

Retailer

Sales

Scientist

TCA

Technical Writer

Technician

Telephone Company

Training

EXERCISES

1. Why are there so many different types of telecommunications personnel?

2. List three types of telecommunications personnel and describe what they do.

3. Why has the military had such a significant impact on telecommunications education and training?

4. How can someone learn telecommunications from books without formal education?

5. How can an English major find employment in the telecommunications field?

6. Why is selling telecommunications equipment and services such a demanding job?

7. Why has the telephone industry been a large employer of telecommunications personnel?

8. Why do government agencies need telecommunications personnel?

9. Contact three telecommunications associations for information on their organizations.

10. Read three telecommunications publications and write a brief description of the topics covered in the publications.

10

The Future

INFORMATION SOCIETY
TECHNOLOGICAL DEVELOPMENTS
LIMITATIONS
TELECOMMUNICATIONS WEB
TELEMARKETING
TELECOMMUTING
KEY WORDS
EXERCISES

Trying to predict the future is always a risky business. Often, the future is not a simple extension of the present. New technological developments can often alter the direction in which a society moves, and these developments can come from unexpected sources.

The transistor, integrated circuits, computers and developments in telecommunications have radically changed American society, yet many of these developments were unanticipated.

This chapter explores some of the emerging trends of society and relates telecommunications to them. It shows some of the possible applications for telecommunications in the future.

INFORMATION SOCIETY

The world is moving toward being an information society. There is a shift—particularly in developed countries—away from manufacturing and toward service economies. Much of this is a radical departure from what has gone on in the past.

Some industries and towns in the U.S. are certainly on the decline. The steel industry is frequently cited as an industry past its prime. Youngstown, Ohio is often considered to be a town fading away with the steel industry.

Since the late 1800s, Youngstown was a vital part of the American steel industry. Whole generations went to work in the steel mills. Wage rates, for even blue collar workers, became respectable. Youngstown was a prosperous steel mill town.

Gradually, though, the steel mills in Youngstown began to close. A tragic scene in the minds of many townspeople was watching no-longer-needed mills being dynamited. In Youngstown today, where the steel mills once stood is empty land. The sky no longer glows red at night from the blast furnaces.

Today, the largest employer in Youngstown is the local university, Youngstown State. As the mills gradually closed, Youngstown State grew and expanded. What in 1960 was a university consisting of only a few buildings is now a university consisting of block after block of buildings. Student enrollment increased from approximately 5,000 students to over 15,000.

Clearly, something significant is happening in America and it is reflected in Youngstown. There has been a decrease in manufacturing industries like steel, but an increase in knowledge industries such as universities.

Many people would say that the U.S. is facing a crisis. However, the Chinese word for crisis is made up of two characters; one stands for danger and the other stands for opportunity. In Youngstown, there has certainly been some of both. There has been the danger of unemployment in the steel mills and the opportunities being offered through the university.

International competition has helped to force the U.S. to look at problems which simply cannot be ignored. The Japanese have been a major competitor. It is not simply a country with a lower wage rate outdoing the U.S.; Japanese products reflect real quality and value.

However, competition is not limited to the Japanese. Many of the products in which they have been so successful—steel, consumer electronics, etc.—are now being produced by other countries. Competition is now a fact of life for everyone, including the Japanese.

Factory automation is playing a large role in the reduction of manufacturing costs and the need for blue collar workers. The Japanese have been among the leaders in the use of robots in factories, and U.S.

companies have been trying to increase their use of robotics and automation. Some factories in both the U.S. and Japan actually have production shifts which are totally automated.

Manufacturing will eventually be like farming in the U.S.; only a small number of people will be needed to produce products. Yet, many new manufacturing companies will continue to come into existence. It still remains relatively simple to start up a company in a garage or basement and then expand it.

Real growth, though, will be in information-related activities. Computers and telecommunications will be two important factors in an information society. Computers are information machines and telecommunications link them to people. Even relatively low-tech operations like selling hamburgers and pizza are becoming computerized and automated. Information of sales, inventory, etc. can be sent to a central computer site via telecommunications on a daily basis. Thus, small operations can have tight control over their operations.

TECHNOLOGICAL DEVELOPMENTS

Many technological developments have been involved in the move to an information society and a service economy. Several of these will be examined in this section.

Electronics will continue to be a key factor. The development of the transistor, integrated circuits, etc. have been and will continue to be important factors in the computer and telecommunications industries.

The lead time for taking technology from the laboratory to full production will continue to decrease. Venture capitalists are interested in financing new technologies, and they will help make new products widely available.

Deregulation will continue to have an impact on telecommunications developments. More companies will see telecommunications as a market for new products and services. There will be an increasing incentive to innovate since entry to this market will be much easier than in the past.

Internationally, many countries are looking at telecommunications in terms of less regulation and more competition. Foreign governments are more fully realizing the importance of technological developments as they relate to telecommunications.

Gradually, computers will be much easier to use (easy as defined by the user and not as defined by computer experts). The telephone is perceived as being easy to operate, and this is the type of operation which users want for personal computers.

The impact of satellite systems on telecommunications has only begun. Satellite earth stations are large complex systems. A new generation of satellite systems with much smaller antennas will enter the market and will help make access to satellites more widely available.

In addition, equipment is being developed for easy communication with satellites from moving vehicles. Today, satellite antennas are carefully adjusted for radio contact with satellites. The new equipment for moving vehicles will not have to be as carefully adjusted for satellite access.

Fiber optics (discussed in Chapter 8) will also become an increasingly important factor for telecommunications, and will be integrated with public telecommunications networks that will provide both home and business users with access to information resources. These networks will provide the same type of distribution routes for the needs of an information society that public highways have provided for a manufacturing economy.

LIMITATIONS

There are certain limitations related to the future which should be understood. All too often it is easy to become blinded by new technological developments and to fail to understand the realities of living in a worldwide economy that involves other people and their objectives.

The U.S. is part of an international economy. This poses limitations that did not exist in the past. Many countries envy the standard of living in the U.S. and other developed nations, and they resent seeing their natural resources being used to keep the U.S., Japan and European nations at a high standard of living at the expense of others. There is no easy answer to this problem.

The ability of the U.S. to see itself as part of an intricate world-wide economy is critical. The U.S. needs foreign markets. Most developed foreign countries—Japan, Sweden, Germany, etc.—are experienced at selling in a world economy. The businesspeople of these countries know how to deal with other countries and have cultivated an understanding of them as people with their own unique economic wants and needs. It is difficult for the U.S.—with its vast internal market—to fully appreciate what it is like to have to sell heavily in a world market.

On a world-wide basis, there are limitations on resources available for economic use. There are also limitations on new sources of capital. While new sources of financing are becoming more widely available, the money supply is not unlimited. Not every idea or product can be financed, and financial people know that despite the enthusiasm of the public for new products and ideas, many of these will fail.

Another limitation is the fact that developmental teams often do not survive from one project to the next. The completion of a large project may result in the break-up of the team responsible for it. Such groups may have unique abilities which are thereupon lost.

Retraining also places a limitation on people resources. It is often easier said than done to retrain people. Retraining requires using skills which may not have been utilized for many years. It may even require forgetting knowledge which is not relevant to current needs. It may also require training for a job which requires adapting to a new culture.

It is easy to talk about retraining a talented worker in a steel mill to repair computers, etc. The reality is that this is often a difficult transition not only in terms of educational demands but also in terms of adapting to a white collar service job.

Management also poses limitations on what any organization can accomplish. Many managers, like people in general, have often had difficulty keeping up with technological developments. It is sometimes difficult for them to appreciate how telecommunications and other technologies can offer real economic and financial advantages to their organizations.

Mergers and management changes impose limitations on the ability of corporations to clearly chart a course which makes the best use of technological innovations and developments.

Many telecommunications and information systems are often large and difficult to manage and develop. Their complexity—which can provide many features and flexibility—can often impose limitations which make it difficult to manage them. Yet, the potential for impressive results is always present.

TELECOMMUNICATIONS WEB

A giant telecommunications web is being created not only in the U.S. but all over the world. While this web is still in the process of being developed, certainly some of its shape and form can be envisioned (Figure 10.1).

This web will be influenced by all that has gone before and what is already in place. It is being affected by the move to an information society and a service economy, and is also being affected by government regulations and the move toward deregulation of equipment and services.

In the workplace there is a move toward office automation. While this trend is still emerging, it appears to involve giving white collar workers increased access to information. In its present form it often involves the

TELECOMMUNICATIONS WEB

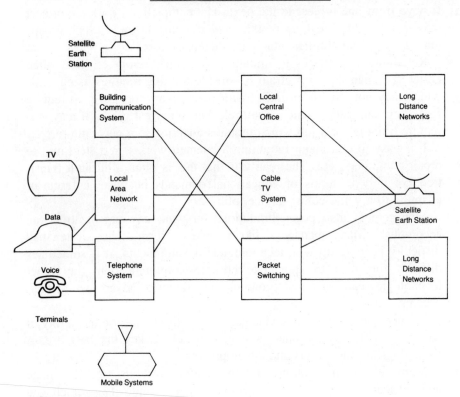

Figure 10.1. In the future, a vast telecommunications web will serve to inter-connect an information-oriented society. _____

use of personal computers, electronic work stations, etc. and the use of telecommunications.

Office automation has been more clearly defined in clerical and administrative tasks which are typically easier to define in terms of their job content and expected performance. Now, the push is toward providing professional workers, analysts, engineers, financial personnel, etc. with increased access to information resources. Regardless of how this is done, it will involve telecommunications.

In some cases, the company telephone will provide access not only for telephone calls but also for some types of message and data communications. Telephone systems of the future will be increasingly digital in nature and have the ability to handle all types of telecommunications.

Within the office there will also be increased use of local area networks for telecommunications applications requiring wide bandwidths and high data-transfer rates. Existing local area networks have been built on coaxial cable technologies; in the future they may rely more on fiber optic cables. There may also be interconnections between local area networks and telephone systems.

The local telephone company central offices will continue to serve within cities and towns. These offices will become increasingly digitized and will offer many new features and services, such as transmitting video pictures.

Other intracity telecommunications will also come into existence. Some may be based on cable television technology. Many local meetings with clients, vendors, etc. may simply be handled via television.

The terminals on office desks will include not only the familiar telephone but will also increasingly include data terminals and terminals for sending and receiving television pictures. Many terminals will be small devices thanks to the increased use of integrated circuits.

Supplementing the traditional long distance networks will be other such networks. Certainly, packet switching networks for message and data communications will become increasingly widespread, and will increasingly have applications developed by trade and user associations. Many problems with speed and data formats will be a thing of the past. Terminal compatibility will be much easier to accomplish.

Satellite antennas at work and home will also become another widely available alternative for many types of long distance telecommunications. They will permit organizations and individuals to have direct access to wide bandwidths of satellite systems.

Some local cable television systems will also have nation-wide coverage to other cities through satellite systems. Opportunities for both traditional and alternative telecommunications vendors will abound.

Mobile telecommunications will become as widespread and sophisticated as that available in an office. People in automobiles will have access to telecommunications not only for telephone conversations but also for message and data communications.

Small hand-held terminals for both the reception and transmission of messages will become widely available. Some will be used for voice communications, others for message and data communications. This will make them suitable for use while riding on public transportation, sitting in public areas, etc. These small terminals will enable people to have quick, easy and silent access to information.

Private networks will still be developed and used by organizations to meet unique needs. They will coexist with public facilities which will be widely available.

At home, individuals will increasingly have the same type of sophisticated access to telecommunications which they have at work. Some of this access will be for business purposes, and most will be for personal use. Most homes will have access to the local telephone company central office, cable television systems, satellite services, etc.

TELEMARKETING

The telecommunications web will be used for many purposes related to the manufacturing, production and distribution of goods and services. In an information society, the marketing of goods and services will become a key activity for many people. Much of this activity will revolve around telemarketing.

The sophistication of future telemarketing activities will surprise many people. Today, telemarketing is still in an embryonic state. It often consists of people trying to sell magazine subscriptions over the telephone. In the future it will be a sophisticated operation serving various markets.

At a basic level, it will provide everyone with access to routine shopping services. Customers will be able to call a store and shop via telecommunications. In some cases they will simply enter orders on a data terminal; in other cases they will be able to see the products via television. They will be able to take a video walk through a store and inspect items and prices. This will save the time and trouble of physically going there. They will make purchases and have them charged electronically to a bank account or credit card. When assistance is needed, the telemarketing shopper will be able to see and talk to a salesperson.

Not all shopping will be done via telecommunications. Customers will still need to visit stores to more closely examine items which are not routine purchases. However, telemarketing walks through the stores will help customers decide which stores to visit, the types of products available, prices, etc. Customers will then be able to make better use of their time once they are in the store.

Even shopping for large items like automobiles may first begin via telemarketing. Computer-controlled systems will answer many routine questions on pricing, options, delivery dates, etc., and a salesperson will provide live interaction when it is needed.

Managers will be able to more quickly adjust their prices and products to meet the competition and demands of the market. Information which may have been difficult or impractical to gather in the past will be readily available via telemarketing. Businesses will do increasingly specialized advertising to attract smaller segments of the market to meet regional trends and preferences.

Research data on customer buying habits will become more widely available. It will be easy to call customers via telecommunications systems to offer new products and services for their unique needs. In some cases, this calling will be done by automated equipment.

Customers will be able to register with central computer data bases regarding products or services in which they have a current or ongoing interest. Then, companies can review this information via telecommunications and contact only those people or organizations who are currently in the market for their products and/or services.

Telemarketing may more physically isolate the buyer and seller from each other, yet it may also help to bring them closer together. It will force people to focus more closely on their needs and products which might satisfy those needs. Telemarketing will revolutionize American buying and selling.

TELECOMMUTING

Many people think that the office of the future will be in their own homes. This is unlikely to happen to the degree that many people envision it, which has more to do with human factors than technology.

Telecommunications *will* enable people to work from their homes. The same sophisticated telecommunications capability available at work will be provided at home if so desired. This will include voice, message, data and video terminals.

In theory, many individuals can do anything at home that he or she can do at work. So, technology will not be the limiting factor. Rather, it will be human and organizational issues that will limit the use of telecommuting.

The U.S. society over the last 100 years has moved away from farming, small shops and individuals who worked close to home to a nation that commutes to work each day. Big business and large organizations have replaced working at home. The introduction of large-scale manufacturing operations played a significant part in this shift in employment patterns.

The move to an information society and a service economy and the widespread use of telecommunications would enable many people to go back to working at home. However, psychologically, many people associate work with a specific place, and it is usually not where they live.

Working also involves more than just work. It involves social contact and interactions with other people. Most people are used to this interaction and would find it difficult to give it up. Working at home can be very lonely and many people could not deal with this.

Some early experiments with telecommuting have involved computer programmers. Often, these people spend much of their day using computer terminals. As a group, they seem comfortable with lower levels of social interaction than other groups of employees. Many programmers may be quite comfortable with telecommuting and working at home. Communicating electronically with their fellow workers may not present significant problems for them. However, other types of people will experience feelings of social isolation.

Working at home requires self-discipline and concentration. The distractions can be tremendous. Unlike farms of the past, a person at home today has many distractions—television, talking to friends on the telephone, etc. The temptations are strong.

The question of how organizations will manage employees who telecommute is complex. Some types of work can be closely measured, while other types of work would be difficult to evaluate from a distance. Also, many managers are motivated by a need for power. This is not necessarily a bad thing, but this need may be thwarted if the people being managed are physically remote from the manager. It may ultimately require the need for different types of managers and supervisors.

How do people get promoted, evaluated, etc. if they are not seen on a regular basis? This involves some new issues which have not had to be faced in the past. Even office politics would take on new directions and meanings in a telecommuting environment. Would those who continue to be physically present each day ultimately have the best chances for promotion?

The reality is that for most employees, for many years to come, telecommuting from home will not be a practical reality for reasons unrelated to technology. However, what will become more of a practical reality is the distribution of employees and functions over a metropolitan area.

Today, in most cities there is a massive flow of people in and out each day. Even organizations with suburban locations have this massive flow to one central point. Telecommunications would make it possible for organizations to have multiple locations within a city to help eliminate this commuting problem.

These distributed work centers would provide the employees a place to go to each day, but it could be a location much closer to where they live. These work centers would provide the structure and peer contact which most people want and need.

This distribution of personnel over multiple locations would be an initial compromise between working at home and working in one central facility. It would serve as a transition point for employees who would eventually work at home, and would increase the organization's familiarity with telecommuting and with using telecommunications to connect the organization and its employees.

In the past, many organizations—particularly large ones—often tried to provide lifetime job security. In recent times, financial difficulties, mergers, competition, etc. have made it increasingly difficult for organizations to provide such security. Being laid off is much more common and socially acceptable.

Just as multiple marriages are increasingly common, so is working for multiple employers. Like it or not, more people in the future will find themselves working for more than one employer over the course of their job careers. Some will become contract employees with no long-term commitments to any one company, and many will eventually work from their homes via telecommunications.

A number of factors will help make this financially possible. Pension plans will become more portable, with contributions by multiple employers counting toward a final pension. Also, the government will continue to encourage people to fund their own pension programs (as with IRAs).

Professional societies and associations will help to provide the type of group access to medical and life insurance which is now usually obtained through employers. So, individuals will increasingly be able to work at home on their own.

Many people feel more loyalty to their profession than to the organizations that employ them. Therefore, the associations may come to provide the type of social network which is today often found within a company.

However, individuals will still have a transitional process in learning how to work on their own. They will have to be able to sell their services on an ongoing basis. This will require tremendous education and retraining, and—somewhat ironically—much of this will be done at home via telecommunications.

KEY WORDS

The reader should be familiar with the following terms in the context in which they were used in this chapter:

Automation

Competition

Crisis

Information Society

Management

Manufacturing

Marketing

Mobile Communications

Office Automation

Public Networks

Regulation

Resources

Satellite Communications

Telecommuting

Telemarketing

EXERCISES

1. Why is there a move toward an information society?

2. Which industries in the U.S. are on the decline and which are on the rise?

3. What have been some of the key technological developments since World War II?

4. How has the field of education been affected by technological developments?

5. Why can every potential product not be developed?

6. What limitations exist on human resources?

7. Why will the existing telephone network not be abandoned?

8. In the future, what goods and services will be available through telemarketing?

9. What impact will telemarketing have on the salesperson's role in society?

10. What are the advantages and disadvantages of working at home?

11. What role will individuals play in future developments of telecommunications?

Bibliography

Aitken, Hugh G. J. *The Continuous Wave*. Princeton, NJ: Princeton University Press, 1985.

Aitken, Hugh G. J. *Syntony and Spark*. Princeton, NJ: Princeton University Press, 1985.

Bone, Jan. *Opportunities in Telecommunications*. Lincolnwood, IL: National Textbook Co., 1985.

Davis, William S. *Information Processing Systems*. Reading, MA: Addison-Wesley, 1979.

Fike, John L. and Friend, George E. *Understanding Telephone Electronics*. Fort Worth, TX: Radio Shack, 1983.

FitzGerald, Jerry and Eason, Tom S. *Fundamentals of Data Communications*. New York: John Wiley & Sons, 1978.

Friend, George E., Fike, John L., Baker, Charles H., and Belamy, John C. *Understanding Data Communications*. Fort Worth, TX: Radio Shack, 1984.

Fuhrman, John C. *Telemanagement*. Englewood Cliffs, NJ: Prentice-Hall, 1985.

Grob, Bernard. *Basic Television and Video Systems*. New York: McGraw-Hill, 1984.

Kiver, Milton and Kaufman, Milton. *Television Electronics*. New York: Van Nostrand Reinhold, 1983.

Martin, James. *Future Developments in Telecommunications*. Englewood Cliffs, NJ: Prentice-Hall, 1977.

Martin, James. *Telecommunications and the Computer*. Englewood Cliffs, NJ: Prentice-Hall, 1976.

Moore, James M. *Radio Spectrum Handbook*. Indianapolis, IN: Howard W. Sams, 1970.

Noll, Edward M. *Broadcast Radio and Television*. Indianapolis: Howard W. Sams, 1981.

Pooch, Udo W., Greene, William H. and Moss, Gary G. *Telecommunications and Networking*. Boston, MA: Little, Brown and Co., 1983.

Shelly, Gary B. and Cashman, Thomas J. *Computer Fundamentals (For an Information Age)*. Brea, CA: Anaheim Publishing, 1984.

Sherman, Kenneth. *Data Communications: A Users Guide*. Reston, VA: Reston Publishing Co., 1981.

Shrader, Robert L. *Electronic Communications*. New York: McGraw-Hill, 1985.

Stamper, David A. *Business Data Communications*. Menlo Park, CA: The Benjamin/Commings Publishing Co., 1986.

Thomas, Ronald R. *Telecommunications for the Executive*. Princeton, NJ: Petrocelli Books, 1984.

Watson, Herbert M., Welch, Herbert E. and Eby, George S. *Understanding Radio*. New York: McGraw-Hill, 1951.

Index

crossbar system, 77
digital, 77
tandem switch, 74
synchronization, 150-154
equalizing pulses in, 153
horizontal-blanking pulse, 153
horizontal-sync pulse, 151
vertical-blanking pulse, 153
vertical-sync pulse, 153
synchronization pulse separator, 156
synchronous transmission, 107, 108
BSC protocol for, 109
error detection techniques for, 110

T

tandem switch, 74
tape drives, 53
technical schools, 199
technological developments, 217-218
technologists, 195, 202
telecommunications
chronology of developments in, 2
codes in, 107
computers' role in, 59-61
divestiture of large holdings in, 2
electricity and electronics as foundation
for, 3
electronic circuits in, 35
industry development in, 1-18
telecommunications analyst, 197
telecommunications business personnel,
198
telecommunications consultants, 197
telecommunications engineers, 196
telecommunications entrepreneurs, 198
telecommunications marketing personnel,
197
telecommunications planners, 197
telecommunications sales personnel, 198
telecommunications scientist, 197
telecommunications technicians, 195
telecommunications web, 219-222
telecommuting, 223-225
telegraph, 2, 4-6
radio vs., 122
trans-Atlantic, 2, 5
transcontinental, 2

Telemarketing, 211
telemarketing, 222-223
telephone, 2, 7-8, 65
automatic exchanges for, 2
cellular, 60
components of, 67
computers use in, 59, 60
dial tone in, 68
diaphragm in, 67
electromagnet in, 67
number pad dialing, 67
ringing in, 68
rotary dial, 67
simple circuit and electrical equivalent
for, 66
store-and-forward systems for, 189
switch hook, 67
transcontinental, 2
telephone systems, 65-91
amplification equipment for, 78
analog vs. digital, 86-88
area codes for, 73
central office in, 68-71
direct current used in, 70
distribution frame for, 68
exchanges in, 72
long distance calling in, 73, 173-179
management and operation of, 70
multiplexing equipment for, 78
numbering system used in, 72
overhead and buried cables for, 77
private, 81-86
ringing current for, 78
sampling, 78
stacking, 78
switchboards, development of, 71
switching equipment in, 69, 70, 73-77
telephone in, 66
transmission equipment in, 70
transmission process in, 77-81
wiring of, 68
Telephony, 210
teleports, 190
teleprinters, 6-7, 104
message communications and, 186
Teletype Corporation, 6
television, 2, 9, 11-13, 147-168